CIPANGO!
(*THE STORY*)

*A brief historical account of the dramatic reversals
in the life of Christopher Columbus, the boldest and
ablest navigator of his time and the embodiment
of the Renaissance spirit of Discovery, who will also be
remembered as the First Immigrant to the "New World"*

ANNE PAOLUCCI

Library of Congress Cataloging-in-Publication Data

Paolucci, Anne
   Cipango! : the dramatic story of Christopher Columbus, who
embodies the spirit of the Renaissance as the boldest navigator
of his time and will also be remembered as the first immigrant
to the "New World" / by Anne Paolucci.
      p. cm.
   ISBN 1-932107-11-8 (alk. paper)
   1. Columbus, Christopher. 2. Explorers–America–Biography.
3. Explorers–Spain–Biography. 4. America–Discovery and
exploration–Spanish. 5. Columbus, Christopher–Fiction.
I. Walter Baehot Council. II. Title.
   E111.P243 2004
   813'.54–dc22

                        2004054026

Published for

THE BAGEHOT COUNCIL

by

GRIFFON HOUSE PUBLICATIONS
P.O. BOX 30727
WILMINGTON, DELAWARE 19805-7727
griffonhse@aol.com

TABLE OF CONTENTS

Columbus is a subject that never goes out of date. He sparks interest on many levels, as well as controversy. This account highlights the drama of his life, the paradoxes and ironic reversals that marked his extraordinary career. Suspicion still lingers about his motives and intentions, his private and public behavior; but in spite of the many questions still raised, he will always be remembered as the embodiment of the Renaissance spirit of adventure and discovery that swept Europe into a new age.

Above: *"The Young Columbus."*
Reproduced from the original
"Age of Discovery Navigators" series of 13
paintings by Constance Del Vecchio Maltese.
(By permission of the artist.)

For Henry

always the master researcher,
the impeccable scholar,
the inspiring writer

Preface

Almost everything that has been said about Columbus, here and elsewhere, has been contested at one time or another. Documents themselves have often proved misleading or ambiguous. It is clear, however, that over the past five centuries enough has been gleaned by researchers, enough evidence has been weighed and scrupulously analyzed many times over, to encourage impeccable scholars like Samuel Eliot Morison, the renowned Paolo Emilio Taviani, and scores of others, to continue exploring the life of Christopher Columbus.

It is a life worth exploring as the many books about him attest. New books continue to be written about him. For this author, the attraction of his life lies in its ironic reversals, the incredible ups and downs he experienced, from the welcome given him in 1493 by King Ferdinand and Queen Isabella on his return from the first momentous journey — a welcome in which Columbus rode in public side by side with the King (something unheard of) — to his humiliating return to Spain, in chains, after the third journey. By the time of his death, in 1506, he was forgotten, cast into a double oblivion.

His frustrations and despair come through, to some extent, in his letters and journals; but until the end of the fourth journey, he never wavered from his goal. The vision that first prompted him to undertake what the ablest navigators of the time did not dare never faltered. He was a man of faith, both Christian faith and faith in his mission. And ultimately, faith in himself, as the man who could realize that mission.

To some, this may have seemed arrogant. Fear or envy made him enemies, even long after his death. He has been accused of heinous crimes, but history cannot be rewritten to suit one's political or social agendas. Conquest has always meant one side wins, the other loses. And the loser is always at the mercy of the conqueror — although perhaps it is less obvious in our day than it was in Columbus's time. And certainly, the age he lived in was, among other things, an age of conquest and expansion. Europe was responding to the urgent need to colonize, to find new trade routes to improve its economy. The desire for information, to learn about the unknown and to re-examine the known, was world-wide. It prodded scientists, writers and artists into new directions, bold discoveries.

Even his enemies would not deny, then or now, that Columbus was by far the ablest navigator of his time, responding, in his own way, to the great changes that were taking place — and not just on the high seas. The age we call Renaissance was at its peak. Genoa herself, and Venice, as the two major long-time seafaring states in Europe, had helped to bring it forth from the tired womb of the Middle Ages.

They were among the first to recognize the new world of economic possibilities by turning their attention more and more to western waters. Florence had been the major financial and cultural architect of the new age, having nurtured exciting new artists like Botticelli and Giotto, the new *dolce stil*, the sweet new style of poetry introduced by Guinizelli, Cavalcanti, and the young Dante, who also gave his native city and the entire Italian peninsula a new language they could call their own, proving his point by deliberately choosing to write his greatest work, *The Divine Comedy*, not in Latin (as Petrarch had chosen to do for what he considered to be his greatest work, *Africa*) but in the Italian vernacular that he had shaped and perfected.

The excitement of this emerging new world burst forth as a celebration of man and his humanity, a new way of paying tribute to God. The world that in the past had been rejected for the promise of eternal life was now rediscovered, a worthy subject for man to study and love. God was boldly worshipped in his creation. It was a compelling and irrevocable reality.

It was also a time of political consolidation after the great struggle between the universal Church of Rome and the universal Empire ruled by the German house of the Hohenstaufens. The Church had won that long struggle, as Dante takes pains to record in many ways in his *Comedy*; but it had emerged weak and unable to defend itself against any upstart force daring to challenge it. The situation is best described by the Latin phrase *terzium gaudens*, "the third party enjoys." What that means in the picture here drawn is that the shattering cataclysmic events that destroyed the old world gave rise to the modern sovereign states of Europe.

Nature abhors a vacuum, the philosophers tell us. An upstart "third party" soon replaced the universal forces that had fought to the point of exhaustion for the "last word" in all matters of rule. The Pope was forced to move from Rome to Avignon, where he served more or less as chaplain to the French King, now the uncontested ruler of the first independent sovereign nation of modern Europe. Germany was not far behind. In Columbus's own time, Spain gained sovereign strength and unity with the marriage of Ferdinand of Aragon and Isabella of Castile.

It was this world of new possibilities, new and exciting challenges that Columbus was launched upon. He is a supreme product of the Renaissance. He challenged the unknown with brazen certainty in his own powers and emerges as the boldest explorer of that incredible age.

Once arrived, however, he discovered there were limits to his powers, victory a fragile prize. In the strange land where he set up the first permanent European colony of the "New World," he suffered privations, prejudice, hatred, and betrayal. He was charged more than once with greed and theft, of plotting against the Monarchs for his own advantage and not following their orders.

This book presents some of the highlights of his incredible story, one which Europeans who crossed the same sea in the last two centuries can relate to easily. It is a story of pride, honor, and loyalty in the face of arduous challenges and many hardships. Twice he had to return to Court to answer charges.

The Queen remained faithful, for as long as circumstances allowed. Her death, two years before that of Columbus, put an end to any hopes that may have lingered in him. In any case, by that time the enterprise had grown so complex, so problematic, that Columbus could not have continued to administer it effectively. In fact, it had become clear, as early as the first voyage, that he had little talent for such work. Even then, with only a relatively small group of men to control, he wasn't able to exert the authority needed to insure the friendship of the natives and to restrain his men from raping and pillaging. His best talents lay elsewhere.

But those talents were no longer required in

the struggle which followed, as the established powers of Europe vied for control of the "New World" he had opened up to them. Having established the route to what was soon recognized as a whole new continent, Columbus's role diminished dramatically, as Spain's control in the area was challenged by Portugal, France, and England, among others — all jostling for position and power.

For better or for worse, history had taken a giant stride forward. But progress is never a simple move forward; it is defined more properly as a series of reversals. Viewed against the inexorable dialectic of history, Columbus's life is a series of contradictions, moving again and again from hope to despair. He reached the pinnacle of success, only to be relegated, in just a few short years, to utter obscurity — even as the land he found was being exploited and colonized by Europe. His death went unnoticed. It was not until centuries later that his exploits were recovered for history, his fame finally assured.

That he made errors is clear; that he is not the monster so often portrayed is also clear. Against the broad background of history, his role is not an aberration, as some critics have insisted. The same Renaissance that gave us magnificent paintings, sculpture, and architecture and set the new parameters of the modern world is also an age of conquest. And conquest more often than not dictates repressive measures, in which the conquered suffer indignities and death. The reality doesn't minimize the enormity of such measures — including using prisoners for hard labor and often, since the time of the Greeks, reducing them to slavery — but history is not advocacy. Nor should it be rewritten to validate personal arguments or to accommodate perceptions of a later age.

There are many controversies still surrounding Columbus. Perhaps they will never be put to rest. My intention in this small volume is neither to denigrate nor exalt him, but to narrate the highlights of his life, without passing moral judgment on his actions or presenting a "case" for or against him. I have not minimized or exaggerated the facts as they have come down to us, nor have I indulged in idle speculation about his intentions or decisions.

———————————

The format of the book — historical narrative in the first part of each chapter, alternating in the second part with a literary narrative based on historical events — is meant to underscore the paradoxes of the story, the reversals of fortune which plagued Columbus from the very beginning of his great adventure.

Some portions of the literary narrative are from dialogue and exchanges originally written for my short play, *Cipango!*, which was staged several times in New York and elsewhere during the "countdown," and, in 1991, was singled out for "official recognition" by the "Christopher Columbus Quincentennial Jubilee Commission" set up by President Ronald Reagan, to mark the 500th anniversary of the landing of Columbus. The play was made into a video in 1990. Though my own creation, the literary narratives are also based on solid research, like the rest of the book.

My most rewarding sources, to which I have returned many times over the years, have been the exemplary works of Paolo Emilio Taviani, the excellent books by Samuel Eliot Morison, the interesting and detailed accounts of Washington Irving (who, while living in Spain, read everything he could get his hands on about Columbus and his time), and the incredibly rich essays on Spain, Italy, Portugal, France and the United States, written by the best scholars of the time, in the more than twenty volumes of that invaluable series, *The Historians' History of the World.*

I would be remiss if I failed to note here the memorable work of Justin Winsor — co-founder of The American Historical Association and the first librarian of Harvard. With the help of other eminent historians, Winsor prepared — as editor-in chief of, and contributor to what Samuel Eliot Morison called "an irreplaceable work" — eight massive volumes, under the title *Narrative and Critical History of America.* The series contains detailed accounts of the early discoveries, descriptions of the indigenous people of the Americas, and much else related to the age of discovery. Some small portions of this incredibly rich source of materials were edited and reproduced in three volumes of *Review of National Literatures* (Council on National Literatures, New York, eds. Anne Paolucci and Henry Paolucci) under the separate titles: *Justin Winsor: Native American Antiquities and Linguistics* (vol. 19, 1996); *Justin Winsor and C. R. Markham, Cultures of the Aztecs, Mayas, and Incas* (vol. 20, 1996); *and Justin Winsor and George E. Ellis: Early Spanish, French, and English Encounters with the American Indians* (vol. 21, 1997).

ANNE PAOLUCCI
February 4, 2004

Above: ""*Amerigo Vespucci.*"
Reproduced from the original
"Age of Discovery Navigators" series of 13
paintings by Constance Del Vecchio Maltese.
(By permission of the artist.)

Chapter One

LOOKING BACK: GENOA?

He has been claimed, at one time or another, by Spain, Greece, England, Corsica, France, Switzerland, and even Portugal, the country first approached and the first to turn down his offer to find for them the short route to Asia by sailing west. The year of his birth has been put forward by some as early as 1441, his death in 1500. To this day, speculation still continues; but the incontrovertible facts that have survived centuries of theories, legends, and unfounded stories are that Cristoforo Colombo, the first man in modern recorded history to cross the vast unknown waters of the western Atlantic, bring back the news, and set up the first permanent colony in this part of the world, was indeed born in Genoa in 1451 (or possibly, somewhat earlier) and died in 1506 in Valladolid, Spain. At the time of his death, he was known as Cristóbal Colón, Admiral of Castilla y León.

The son of Domenico Colombo and his wife Susanna Fontanarossa, Columbus already was sailing the high seas by the time he was fifteen. The merchant ships on which he served took him, between 1474 and 1476, to China, the Aegean Sea, and into Tunisian waters.

Soon after, a Genovese ship he was on, bound for England, was attacked by a French Corsair fleet under the command of Guillaume Casenove, or Coulon le vieux — a name which later surfaced as another version of "Colón," and which suggested to some scholars a family connection (unfounded) and further confused the issue of his birth. The ship was sunk by the French off Cape St. Vincent, but Columbus managed to swim to safety near Lagos and from there found his way to Lisbon. From Lisbon, he sailed to Bristol, England (1476), then to Iceland. By 1477, he was back in Lisbon, where he had decided to settle down.

Fate decided otherwise. In the summer of 1479, he visited Genoa briefly (very likely his last visit to his native city), to testify in a suit for non-payment of a shipment of sugar he had purchased in Madeira the previous year, for a client. He stayed just long enough to testify, then told the authorities that he had to "leave the next day" on urgent business. Whether or not he really had pressing reasons for rushing back to Lisbon is uncertain, but he did have other things on his mind. He had decided to marry. The woman he had chosen to marry was Felipe Moniz de Perestrello, daughter of the first governor of Porto Santo. The wedding took place soon after his return from Genoa, and the young couple then moved to Porto Santo, where they set up their first home and where their son Diego was born.

Although he had remained a Genovese citizen until then, he chose, with his marriage, to become a naturalized Portuguese subject through his wife Felipe. The change in status was not a casual decision: he was prepared to become a Portuguese for at least two important considerations. The first was that his father-in-law, Bartolomeo Perestrello, had inherited patents of nobility conferred on the family by the Portuguese king. Felipe herself could claim even more impressive noble lineage through her mother's family. To Columbus, who aspired to gain some kind of title for himself as well as for his brothers and his children, this was a welcome bonus — indeed, to some critics, an essential condition for the success of the marriage. Just as important was the fact that, years earlier, Felipe's father had been chosen by the Portuguese king to govern the island of Porto Santo, not too far from Madeira. When Bartolomeo died, the royal assignment had passed to his son. Bartolomeo had not been a seafaring man (contrary to many stories that surfaced over the years); but the fact that the king had put him in charge of what was an important base for Portuguese explorations into the Atlantic, and that charge was now held by Columbus's new brother-in-law, was a reality not to be minimized. The family connection with the king, together with the fact that the Portuguese were the best trained and most experienced seamen of the time and had the best equipped ships, would also serve him well.

Portugal had earned the reputation of being the most forward-looking, progressive of the sea-faring nations of this time — thanks to the keen interest of Prince Henry "The Navigator," who had followed maritime activities closely, particularly exploration along the western coast of Africa. That same interest found a ready subject in King João (John II), who held the throne at the time Columbus first devised his plan to sail west. Under this king, Portugal continued to forge ahead in its quest for new trade routes.

It would have been unrealistic for Columbus to ignore the full implications of his marriage to Felipe. It spelled a rare advantage, not the least of which was an important connection at Court. Was it the reason for the marriage? Witnesses of the event tell us that was definitely not the case, that the marriage to Felipe was not to be interpreted in any way as opportunistic. It had been a love match, as Columbus himself was to assert, much later, to his son Diego.

From his home base in Porto Santo, Columbus continued to take on commissions and sailed on commercial vessels to the Canaries and the Azores. Between 1482 and 1483, he visited the Portuguese fort of São Jorge de la Mina in Guinea, passing the Cape Verde Islands on his way back. By now he was clearly established as a reputable sea captain with many years of experience on the high seas. He could easily have settled down to that life — enjoying his home and family between trips, and studying at leisure the charts, maps, and documents of his father-in-law's rich library.

But stirrings of the great Adventure were already forcing his attention elsewhere.

The first sign of the bold plan that was shaping inside him was the correspondence he initiated and continued between 1481 and 1482 with the renowned Florentine cosmographer, Paolo Toscanelli. Perhaps he had confided earlier, to friends, on his brief visit to Genoa, something of what was germinating inside him; he may even have broached the idea to the Genovese authorities or the people he knew at Banco di San Giorgio, which financed many shippers. If so, there is no record to support the notion. More likely, Columbus realized during that visit to Genoa, even earlier perhaps, that his native city was in no position to finance any expedition of the kind he had in mind. He must have grasped, once and for all, that there was no future for him there. Genoa had suffered a decline; there was no financial support to be found there now, just as it did not offer any promise earlier. Wasn't that the reason he had left, as so many others had, including his older brother Bartholomew: to seek a better life, better opportunities elsewhere?

His marriage to Felipe redefined the parameters of his personal future.

His correspondence with Toscanelli opened up the new route he was to trace for himself as a man dedicated to the sea and to discovery.

From this point forward, the story of Columbus becomes a series of ironic twists and turns, a tale of tremendous exaltation and short-lived victories, a Sophoclean juxtaposition of incredible successes and devastating despair. Throughout, his plans were threatened and thwarted by the doubts, envy, and prejudices of others. Repeatedly, his hopes were shattered,

19

much like the giant waves and hurricane winds of the Caribbean destroyed his ships and left him and his crew stranded in Jamaica, on ships no longer seaworthy, at the end of his fourth and last journey to the "New World" he had opened up for an expanding Europe.

The Queen, he knew, was no longer there to support him. He waited now simply to be rescued, but even that seemed a far-fetched hope. By then he had come to see clearly that his part in the escalating enterprise he had begun was over. What he probably did not grasp, then or later, was the full extent of what he had done.

LOOKING AHEAD: STRANDED IN JAMAICA

"They're at it again?"

It was Mario, one of the boys, who presumed to give voice to what the rest of the men were thinking. They had all gathered around the entryway to the Admiral's quarters, having heard the angry voices, not wondering any more about where it was all leading but worrying, instead, about what they knew perfectly well was bound to happen to them. They had no illusions.

Carlo, the second quartermaster, turned to the boy, a child really, related in some way to a distant cousin of Columbus's late wife. His harsh look registered displeasure. His brows furrowed into deep ridges as he studied the youngster briefly, but there was also resignation and fear in his eyes. Something of the deep-seated anxieties in that gaze, an unspoken knowledge that most of the seasoned crew seemed to share, communicated itself to the boy. He stumbled back, confused, uncertain about the meaning of that look, although even at the age of eleven he understood enough to know that they were all in deep trouble, had been, since the two remaining ships of the several furnished to the Admiral for this fourth voyage had been forced to seek haven here, after the terrible storms they had encountered. And here they still were, not daring to go ashore, where the natives watched them day and night, venturing closer and closer to the helpless ships with each passing day, as though waiting for the right moment to rush aboard and kill them all.

By this time it was clear, even to young Mario, that the ship and all who were left on board were in grave danger. The ships, of course, were no longer seaworthy after eighty-eight days of hellish storm, winds the likes of which, the Admiral himself had admitted, he had never experienced before! They had been exploring the vast sea between Paria and Hispaniola when the storms began. The ships strained against the mighty winds that swept them away from their home base to this other island west of it, a large body of water between them.

They were stranded there, with no possibility of letting others know where they were. Those waiting for their return had probably given them up by now. Who could possibly imagine they were sill alive, waiting to be rescued?

After weeks of waiting, without any sign of rescue (how could they be rescued when no one even knew where to look?), sickness and depression began to take their inevitable toll. It was then that Diego Mendez, loyal faithful Diego, had volunteered to raise a sail on one of the large Mayan canoes they had brought back with them, and, with a few supplies from their almost depleted stores, try to cross the treacherous waters between this island and Hispaniola, to let the governor know they were still alive.

He was a strong and capable seaman. He took on

21

the assignment with simple but forceful words and the authority of experience.

"We're not at risk, Admiral," he said without any preamble, "we're at death's door. Those of us who won't die of starvation or disease will be killed by the natives. Our supplies will soon be gone, the natives are waiting for just the right moment to storm what's left of these poor wrecks. I will try my best to get across. It's our only chance —"

Moved by the man's unwavering commitment and loyalty, Columbus turned away. Diego waited as the Admiral slowly straightened his shoulders and cleared his throat. They both knew he would never have given such an order had there been any other possible way out of their predicament. It was a last desperate attempt, all the odds against its succeeding. Everyone knew that even a sturdy boat could get crushed like a toy in the kind of weather they had come through. And there was plenty of it to worry about there.

"You know what lies ahead. . . ." It was not a question, but a sad reminder of the hazardous journey that very likely would claim the man's life. The memory of what they had suffered in those terrible storms rose up between them, all too vivid, even more frightening at this distance than when they were busy struggling to get through them.

"Sir, I welcome death at sea, if that is my fate."

Columbus put his hand on the man's shoulder. "Knowing what the seas here are like, everything in me wants you not to go; but as your commander I am bound to do what is necessary. I give the order with a heavy heart, but if there's even a slight chance you can reach Hispaniola and get help, I cannot ignore that possibility. The fate of all of us will be in your hands." Spontaneously, he embraced the man. "God go with you, then."

That was a year ago.

At the time, Mario had fought back the tears of

22

relief that threatened to spill over. For weeks, he continued to pray to St. Nicholas and other worthy saints to help Diego reach Hispaniola, so that they could all see Spain and their loved ones again.

Those who had lived long enough to read the signs of destiny were not optimistic, although they too prayed, each in his own way. For them too, Diego's departure had been the occasion of renewed hope. Even the Admiral had been seen to smile, now and then. But the older members of the crew whispered when alone, among themselves, that the odds that Diego would reach Hispaniola were slim indeed, and that they had probably all been given up months ago, as lost at sea, forgotten by now. Even if some few continued to miss them and still wondered about their fate, where would they begin to look for them, given the chance? How could anyone guess they were stranded on ships no longer fit even to live on? That after miraculously living through eighty-eight horrendous storms of unimaginable strength, winds of such magnitude that just thinking about them made them tremble, they had been forced to this shore, to wait for death? Diego was a long shot, but he was their last and only hope.

Watching the silent men standing warily as the voices rose and swelled into curses and shouting, Mario began to understand the serious concerns of those around him. Something of their silent despair reached inside him and clutched at his young heart. He felt he was smothering and quickly moved down the uneven splintered deck, treading carefully around the holes and the worm-eaten rotting planks. He too must be strong, he reasoned, follow the example of the other crew members. As he edged his way toward the rail, a wave of unhappiness overwhelmed him, and he felt tears blurring his vision and running down his cheeks. Quickly he rubbed his eyes with his closed fists, a familiar childhood gesture. He thought of his mother, who

23

had pampered him with his favorite dishes, his brother Tonio, who was apprenticed to a silversmith and was ready to marry soon. How he missed them!

No one seemed to have noticed the tears. But the quiet resignation of those around him had its effect on the boy. He sniffed, pulled back his head, closed his eyes. Slowly he moved back to the edge of the group crowded around the entryway. He wasn't really interested in the quarrel between the Admiral and his second in command. He needed to be near the others, even though his attention was claimed by the pictures in his head – those unpredictable waters that no doubt had claimed Diego by now, the fate that lay ahead for all of them, the natives watching them, each day drawing closer. What if they rushed on board, some night, as they slept? They ate human flesh, he had heard.

An involuntary shudder passed through him. He felt cold suddenly. One way or another all of them would soon be swallowed into oblivion.

Something crashed inside the Admiral's cabin. The men quickly dispersed as the second in command strode out, The Admiral could still be heard shouting in the wake of the other's retreat. The man, still strong but wild-eyed and haggard from worries and privation, lashed out at them, anger and frustration finding a ready target.

"Lazy good-for-nothings! Why aren't you at your posts?" They all knew, of course, there was not much to do. God knows they were more than willing to work all day, every day, into the night even, if the ships could be repaired, if they could go ashore and cut down the timber needed to replace the planks and masts and all the rest that had been damaged. But they all knew that if they ventured out there, none of them was likely to be seen again. Several men had already been lost to the natives. Besides, most of their instruments had also been damaged and were no longer

24

working. How could they hazard a trip back to Hispaniola on these poor shells that the forces of nature had stripped and battered? Still, they had been given tasks to keep busy. They started to move away, their captain pushing aside those nearest him with a heavy arm, shoving others to the right and left, as he strode past. The men scattered.

Inside his quarters, Columbus crossed his arms on the table in front of him and wearily rested his head on them. He prayed silently for the strength to control his temper, to stem the recriminations that echoed in his head. His hands still trembled from the force of the quarrel. He vowed to make it up to the captain he had berated. God help him: the storms had battered their souls as well as the ships, they were all on edge. He wasn't helping them any. His men were resigned to the inevitable, but fear tugged at their resignation and threatened to take away the last vestiges of courage. Quarreling only made matters worse. He should not have taken his own frustrations out on the captain. He should think of the men, help them face the ordeals that loomed ahead, instead of scolding and shouting. . . .

Was this really the end, then? All his efforts come to nothing? Such closure, abandoned and forgotten, was painful to contemplate. Surely God would hear his prayers!

Maybe Diego had reached Hispaniola, after all!

Maybe it was just a matter of time –

Maybe they would be rescued. . . .

His mind lingered briefly on those improbable conjectures, rejected them even as he rose and prepared to go on deck. Whatever his doubts, he knew he must hide them from the others. It was up to him to set an example, even now, especially now, under these impossible circumstances –

It was up to him to give his men the courage to die.

His heart ached.

Would he ever see his sons again?

25

Chapter Two

THE HISTORIC FIRST JOURNEY

Isabella has gone down in history as having been an active and effective head of state. Together with Ferdinand, she brought the country out of the chaos of the Moorish wars, tapping new energies Spain had been unaware of before. Under the joint rule of these two monarchs, the country added to its resources, expanding domestic industry and trade as well as commercial ventures abroad. A new age had emerged; Spain felt and responded to the spirit of enlightenment that encouraged cultural, scientific, and other intellectual interests.

Having built a prosperous economy now able to compete with the other nations of Europe, Spain had at the same time acquired and consolidated some of the most important territories in Europe and Africa. By the time Columbus set out on his first voyage, the country had regained a good measure of prosperity and prominence.

It was primarily Isabella's doing. She ruled with a practical sense of the possibilities ahead and did not shy away from hard decisions. Her first efforts were directed at reforming the nobility and curbing their quarrelsome spirit. She was just as determined — notwithstanding her deep attachment to the Catholic faith — to resist any encroachment on her government by the Church. She did more than any other of her predecessors to reform the habits of the clergy and to restrict their powers.

To her great credit, she also gave all citizens the chance to better themselves, and those who succeeded were properly rewarded, no matter how humble their place in life. New avenues of wealth and honors were opened to everyone; persons as well as property were protected under her fearless and impartial administration of justice.

In all things, the Queen, unlike her cold, calculating, and suspicious husband, displayed a spirit of generosity and high-mindedness, as well as dedication to the interests of her country and people. It must be added, to her great credit, that she remained loyal and true to the King, who was less than her equal in habits and character. Isabella did not indulge any of the petty artifices connected with Court politics; unlike Ferdinand, she was bent on achieving only the most honorable ends with the best means at hand. In character, competence and vision, she stands far above her age.

By the time Columbus appeared on the scene, Isabella had effected great changes and improvements. New laws had been passed that encouraged foreigners to settle in Spain; laws that encouraged the expansion of means of communication and travel, including canals, harbors, and bridges; laws that improved city facilities; laws that relieved people from paying heavy tolls and also freed them from oppressive monopolies; laws that established a uniform currency, and a standard form of weights and measures for the entire kingdom, laws that resulted in the restructuring and maintenance of an orderly and efficient police force, which gave Spain the reputation of being the safest country in Europe. Laws also were passed that induced even the common man to put money in useful enterprises; for the terms of all contracts were now made binding and had to be honored. These measures effectively restored public confidence and trust, the true basis of public cooperation in the economic life of a state.

It was this reconstituted Spain which Columbus sought out to sponsor his bold plan. It was the only nation he had approached that did not categorically dismiss his notion that he could find a short western route to the Indies and the Far East by sailing west. It was the enlightened patronage of Isabella that made possible the realization of Columbus's risky enterprise.

Still, it took seven years for her to come to a decision and act on it.

During that time, there had been much controversy among the learned men at Court about the feasibility of the plan Columbus had described. Some called it insane. Others were suspicious of the man himself, the foreigner from Genoa, who had left his land of birth and his family to find wealth and success elsewhere. Still others considered him, more properly, Portuguese, since he had married a Portuguese woman, as his older brother Bartholomew had before him, and spoke and wrote in that language. In either case, he was not to be trusted.

Columbus suffered all this in silence, putting up with insults and doubts as to his sanity. Even children in the streets mocked him. His appearance suffered as well: his clothes had grown worn and shabby, but he didn't have the means to replace them. If, during this time, he had any thoughts of giving up in the face of all these difficulties, he gave no outward sign. Nor did he ever doubt the outcome of his proposed journey. In public, he was careful not to show his impatience, deferring to the priorities the King and Queen had set for themselves. He understood, in spite of delays that tortured him, that they had much else to deal with, before they could turn their attention to his project.

But the waiting grew oppressive. Many who heard about his plan said it was a wild idea, . . . but what if by some miraculous trick of fate he did succeed in crossing that unknown sea and reach Asia? The prospect was mind-boggling. Spain would have first claim to the route he would have charted and in no time could reap incredible riches. Spain's future would be insured, her enemies rendered helpless against her new wealth and influence.

Columbus shrugged off rumors and idle speculation. For him, the plan was anything but mind-boggling. His calculations indicated clearly that he could reach the outer islands of Cipango by sailing west. And just beyond those islands was Asia. It was simply a matter of crossing that large sea, of having the courage to persevere and sail westward until they reached land again.

It *had* to be there. Everything pointed to it. It could be done; it *would* be done. He had all the maps, charts, tables, ready to show and explain to anyone who would listen. All he needed was the support of the Monarchs. It would be an arduous journey, a long one, but he wouldn't give up, turn back the way the Portuguese had done. He was not afraid. The important thing was that the King and Queen had not dismissed the idea. He was certain when the time came they would approve it. His long waiting would pay off.

It was during this time of waiting that his Portuguese wife Felipe died. Now in Spain, and perhaps thinking that his future lay there, Columbus formed a relationship with a Spanish woman called Beatrix Enriquez. She eventually bore him a son, but they never married. It proved to be a lasting relationship. Columbus remained loyal to Beatrix to the very end of his life; their son Fernando was as dear to him as his legitimate son, Diego.

At one point, growing more impatient as weeks and months slipped by, Columbus had his brother Bartholomew and some prominent friends once more approach the King of Portugal, as well as King Henry VII of England with his plan. Both sovereigns showed interest in the idea put forward to them, but Columbus quickly aborted those possibilities when Spain gave him fresh assurances and promises. By 1490, however, after waiting five years for the Sovereigns to turn their attention to his project, Columbus forced a decision. The result was a terrible blow. The Sovereigns made clear that everything else had to wait until the wars they were fighting came to an end.

Dejected at having wasted so many years, his meager resources gone, Columbus left, taking with him his son Fernando. He found temporary refuge in the Franciscan monastery of Santa Maria de Rabida. The prior of the place, Juan Perez de Marchena, an intelligent and cultured man, soon realized that the weary, poorly-dressed man who had stopped to ask for some bread and water for his young son was a well-read, experienced sea captain.

When he heard what had happened and about the plan Columbus had put forward at Court, Perez decided to help. First he invited a number of prominent men of the area to meet Columbus. One of these was Martín Pinzón, a wealthy and prosperous businessman and shipowner. This was the first encounter between Columbus and the man who would soon share his destiny and accompany him in the historic voyage to the New World.

Perez, who had contacts at Court, then wrote to the Queen, asking her to reconsider her decision and call back Columbus. Isabella, who had always favored Columbus and was one of his staunchest supporters, was indeed ready to reconsider her decision and invited him to return to Court. The timing couldn't have been better. The Moors had just surrendered their last stronghold, Granada. The wars were over.

He had, during the years of waiting at Court, spent much of the time perfecting himself in Spanish, so that, when the call came, he would be able to make his case directly and fluently before the Monarchs and the Spanish dignitaries who would assemble to hear his arguments. He knew, given the chance, he could convince them. The day had come to make his case.

His task was not an easy one. To be sure, cosmographers and seafaring men understood him; they could relate to what he had to say, in terms familiar to them. Not that their common interests precluded objections on the part of those who were thus equipped to follow him more easily in his arguments. He could handle their questions. The problem was answering the theologians, who found objections to the idea in many passages of the Bible.

Columbus found himself forced into explicating biblical texts which, taken literally, seemed to undermine his premises and his observations about the land and sea.

There were also some who went so far as to insist that Columbus was keeping back some important information, that he knew more than he was telling them. Rumor had it that he had waited those seven years at Court, struggling to keep up, often having to rely on his friends for even the barest necessities, because he had an ace up his sleeve: secret information from a shipwrecked sailor he had saved at sea about unexplored land to the west. His enemies were quick to accuse Columbus of holding back that information so that he could build up the dangers of the proposed journey and thereby raise the stakes and claim a heroic reward when he succeeded. Nothing has ever been found to support this rumor.

The King and Queen followed the debates among the learned men who had been invited to Court for consultation. They, like the astronomers, cosmographers, and theologians who had assembled to hear Columbus explain his plan, were impressed by his enthusiasm and struck by his determination, by his almost reckless faith in the conclusions he had reached. Whatever happened, he certainly would not turn back, like the Portuguese had.

The crucial arguments were those of the theologians. The Sovereigns listened closely to what they had to say, for their objections could not be minimized or readily dismissed. But always, in the back of their minds, was the lure of the unimaginable possibilities that lay in store for Spain, if Columbus did indeed find land at the end of his journey westward.

It was also in keeping with her spirit of inquiry and enlightenment that Isabella finally decided they should support the plan. She had already and in many ways shown herself to be a ruler with vision, as well as a practical and effective one; her decision (for it was hers more than the King's) to underwrite the hazardous journey described by Columbus strengthened that reputation. In her realistic perception of things, she saw the project Columbus proposed as an incredible incentive, a challenge not to be ignored. Besides, Portugal had already proved to be a dangerous competitor. Hadn't the

Portuguese tried to murder Columbus, to get him out of the way? Hadn't they stolen his charts and maps, all the careful notes he had prepared, using them to venture out secretly into that unknown ocean sea, only to be overcome with fear and turn back? Sooner or later they might risk it again, or some other country might.

Still, it was a long shot. When the time came to commit themselves, the Sovereigns were cautious. Their support turned out to be a small investment in the end. They provided Columbus with royal letters to facilitate his raising of funds, ships and equipment. They also gave direct orders to the citizens of the small port of Palos to fit out, within two months' time, two caravels and to find men, supplies, and materials for the two ships. The Crown would pay the wages for a crew, as well as a four-month advance. But a crew was almost impossible to round up, so the Sovereigns announced that those men in the jails who signed up for the expedition would have all criminal charges against them dropped. Only four prisoners took up the offer. Many more convicted prisoners would be pressed into service for the subsequent journeys — an action Columbus would later regret. The city itself, in exchange for its cooperation, would be excused from paying fines it had incurred.

While these preparations were under way, Columbus accepted the offer of a ship, the Gallega, from a friend, Juan de la Cosa, who was also prepared to sail along with Columbus as captain of the vessel. Later renamed the Santa Maria, Columbus chose it as his flagship. But getting men and supplies became a large problem. In spite of the royal orders, the people of Palos were skeptical of the plan that had been described and suspicious of Columbus, who was a total stranger to them. Why should they trust him? Besides, even the most experienced sea captains considered the idea foolhardy. Why take such a risk?

It was at this point that Martín Pinzón, who had first met Columbus at La Rabida, reappears to help him. He offered Columbus two ships, as he had promised when they had first met. The two men had struck it off, back then, each recognizing in the other a kindred spirit, someone familiar with the sea, whose experience and intelligence would understand what was at stake and how best to achieve it. Abandoning his usual caution, Columbus had confided his plans to Pinzón, who had expressed enthusiasm and promised his full support. Now, true to his word, he not only provided two ships but also went about getting men and supplies for them.

An experienced sea captain himself, as well as a man of reputation and means, Pinzón used his considerable influence and reputation to recruit the full quota of men needed. He had no trouble doing so. He then turned to the task of assembling all that was needed to furnish the ships for the journey ahead. This too he accomplished without difficulty. He himself would be in charge of the Pinta; his brother

Vincente would sail on the Niña.

This moment is the most optimistic, the most honest and hopeful, in the relationship of the two men. We see Pinzón at his best: the willing and cooperative partner, the confident sea captain. We see Columbus grateful, ready to trust him. Still, it would have been naive for either of them not to consider their own personal motives, their aspirations, the wealth and honors that would be theirs, if all went well. Who could fault them for entertaining such hopes?

Pinzón had come through as he had promised. Columbus gratefully acknowledged that his new partner had proved himself true and worthy. There was no reason to question ulterior motives and actions yet to come. Besides, other matters occupied them as they made their final preparations.

The long waiting had drained Columbus in every way. Now, with departure imminent, he had to face the hard reality of sailing from the small port of Palos. None of the major ports were available to him; they were being put to more pressing service. The Sovereigns had made clear, with the end of the Moorish wars: that they would not tolerate non-Christian influences. The Jews were the main targets. Unless they converted to Christianity, they had to leave Spain. Some Jews submitted, others chose to leave and were soon dispersed, many stranded in places that were inhospitable, a large number killed by the strangers who would not accept them. It was an old story. Later, the

Muslims living in Spain would be forced out in the same way. Their fate was perhaps even more dreadful than that of the Jews, for they had limited resources and more enemies in what was essentially a non-Arab, non-Muslim world.

In this connection, Isabella had given Columbus strict orders, consistent with her edicts against the Jews and Muslims. Any natives encountered in his journeys were to be converted to Christianity and, she insisted, as Christians, should not be used for forced labor or sold into slavery. Circumstances would work against her decision. When there were not enough of his own men to work the fields and the mines, Columbus was forced to use the Indians for those tasks. Later, when the promised gold did not materialize, he sold Indians in order to make up for the treasure he could not deliver. Others who came after him, with only personal greed as their motive, had no scruples continuing the practice.

Slavery was a new phenomenon in this part of the world; but the practice dates back as least to Greek times, when those captured in war became slaves of the victors. It continued into Roman times and right up to the present. Today, in spite of centuries of enlightened reforms, slavery still exists in places like Africa.

To Columbus, sailing out on that first journey, the task of converting the natives, as the Queen had ordered, must have seemed secondary in the light of the major premise. He did not object to the conditions Isabella had set forth. They seemed simple enough.

He would soon learn otherwise. But at that moment, his overriding concern was the journey he had planned for so long.

They sailed from Palos on Friday, August 3, 1492.

The quarrels with Pinzón started almost immediately.

At first, Columbus ignored Pinzón's arrogance, his reminders that he had been instrumental in making the voyage possible, that the Pinta (on which he sailed) and the Niña (in the charge of his brother Vincente) were his ships, that he commanded at least the same respect and authority as Columbus. He resented his decisions being overruled, questioned the judgment of the Admiral. Columbus tolerated this for a while. After all, he had the last word. The Queen had given him full authority; he had papers that proved it. So he tried to ignore the veiled insults, the questions, the suspicions. But the crew were beginning to notice, and Pinzón's criticism might indirectly or even deliberately encourage them to turn against him.

It was clear that the man had an agenda of his own. His mind was fixed on the gold waiting out there, the treasures he would bring back for himself. He was also bent on getting at least some of the many honors and privileges Columbus now enjoyed, even if it meant doing everything possible to undermine him at Court and finding opportunities to erode his authority — the man whom the Queen had trusted to be in charge of the small fleet.

Toward that end, he would watch him

falter, catch him in some error. It soon became obvious that Pinzón's plan was to report back to the Sovereigns anything that would show the Admiral weak, uncertain, lacking the strength to move forward, incapable of carrying out the charge entrusted to him.

Columbus tried hard to avoid quarreling with Pinzón. Instead, he kept careful notes of all his actions, all the data necessary to justify his decisions, if necessary. Information was properly recorded, so that it could not be challenged later. He tried very hard to control his temper.

Clearly, Pinzón had become a threat, not only to Columbus, personally, but also to the success of the enterprise. His behavior was affecting those around him. The length of the voyage was already causing the men to grumble. Pinzón's attitude did not help. When the men threatened to mutiny, Columbus used every argument he could muster to calm them. Had they not reached land when they did, his crew very likely would have killed him.

MARTÍN PINZÓN

The quarrels had begun soon after they sailed. They continued after landfall, on that incredible twelfth day of October. They grew more frequent, until one day, Pinzón lifted anchor and took off on his own, without telling anyone where he was going. Days and weeks went by. At first Columbus was worried, then stunned at such a betrayal. Worry quickly overwhelmed all other emotions that had risen like bile to poison his trusting nature. Pinzón had left them with only one ship, the smallest, the Niña, to hazard back on, the Santa Maria having been wrecked on a sand-bank soon after Pinzón disappeared. How could they return safely to Spain with only one small ship, without any back-up?

The loss of the Santa Maria had been hard to bear. The incident was a bitter memory that Columbus could not erase from his memory. It was not the usual accident; it need not have happened. He had always been firm and explicit about not leaving the inexperienced boys in charge of the tiller or entrusted with the helm. On the night of December 25, Columbus had gone below to get some sleep. The Master, who earlier had steered the ship back from two days of exploring nearby islands, also went below to get some rest, leaving the tiller in charge of one of the boys – what the Admiral had expressly forbidden. But the Master was tired and saw no harm in putting the boy in charge on such a calm night, the sea as smooth as glass.

While the others slept, the inexperienced lad did not realize that the ship had drifted on to a sand-bank. By the time he gave the alarm, the ship was tilting. All efforts to lighten her and pull her off were in vain. Columbus gave the Master some orders, but the man took off for the Niña instead, hoping for refuge there. The captain of the Niña prudently refused him permission to board. The man was forced back; but the Niña's boat arrived first, only to find that the Santa Maria had gone aground and was taking in water.

All efforts to lighten the ship failed to free her. She soon fell on her side and began to break up. With the help of friendly natives, Columbus and his men worked through the night and into the next day to salvage as much as they could from the wrecked ship. He assigned some of his men to guard what they had unloaded, until they could store it safely elsewhere. The only good that came out of the disaster was that the wood recovered from the wrecked ship was put to use to build their first fort, La Navidad.

Three weeks after he had left them, Pinzón suddenly turned up again. He had found little to show for his defection, made no excuses, showed no regret for putting their lives in danger, and was no less contentious.

Now they sat opposite one another, in the Admiral's cabin. Suspicion lay heavy between them. He had vowed not to lose his temper. If he did, if he stormed out or ignored the man (he would have loved to do just that!), it would simply give Pinzón something else to report against him at Court. No, he would make every effort to be discreet, affable even, if at all possible.

He had pulled out his charts and maps and had begun to trace the return route he proposed they take.

"What are you worried about?" Columbus asked, as Pinzón shook his head. "My dead reckoning has never failed us, has it? Besides, you said yourself, no one can read maps and charts as well as I do. I got us here, didn't I?"

"You changed course too many times —"

"I've kept careful notes," Columbus said, as he unrolled another map. He traced with his finger as he went on: "From Palos, south to the Canaries." He looked up and met the other's impatient gaze. "Surely you don't question my judgment there!"

"No. The Pinta needed a new rudder. We would have lost her and perhaps the other two ships as well if we hadn't stopped there. But going through that sea of weeds? We could have been sucked into it! You should not have lingered. But you insisted. 'No,' you said, 'I must take notes,' you said. Meantime the waters thickened, the vegetation threatened to choke us. The ships could hardly move. We could have been drowned! What good would all your notes have been, then, eh? You put us all at risk, there! And what about your crazy reading of the stars?"

Columbus could not hide his annoyance.

"My readings were accurate enough! And the sea of weeds was a phenomenon worth exploring."

"The delay could have cost us our lives. But you wouldn't listen to reason!"

"Have you forgotten that exploration is part of the charge given me? Keeping careful records is part of it. In this case, my notes were crucial. They will establish the route for future trips. They will help correct the charts and maps we now have. That sea of weeds has been the source of horror stories for too long. I will have destroyed those myths –"

"You will have proved that you put us all at risk!"

"It had to be done!" Pinzón said nothing. Columbus went on, after an awkward pause: "I would certainly have resumed course quickly, if I had thought that was true. It was only a brief delay. My judgment proved correct."

"Ah, your infallible judgment!"

"All right, I admit it was a mistake to turn northward, when the men almost convinced me that there was land there."

Pinzón pushed back his chair and crossed his legs. He studied the other man briefly, then cocked his head to one side, as though harboring a secret. A small smile hovered on his lips.

"You're always so sure of yourself! You pour over Toscanelli's maps – Toscanelli, mind you, the greatest authority in these matters – then say they aren't exactly accurate and decide to sail west, west, west, then north, then southwest." He rose to stand behind his chair, his hostility manifesting itself in every movement of his rigid body, his twitching lips, as well as in the rising pitch of his voice. *"You and your charts! You must have changed course at least five times. What kind of plan is that? In the end, you followed a flock of birds!"* His voice had grown louder, his tone bitter, his face flushed, fresh anger welling up inside him, as it

42

always did when he remembered the Admiral's stubborn insistence on having his way.

Columbus frowned. He was beginning to lose patience. "Listen, friend! I had to rely on all my skills as a navigator, all that was here in my brain" – pointing to his head – "all my charts, notes, maps, all my experience with currents, the movements of the stars, signs of every kind – water, winds, everything – trusting to instinct a good deal of the time, yes! and to birds! The proof is, we have reached land! I got us here. Isn't that enough for you?"

"According to your . . . log – ?"

The question hovered unpleasantly between them. Both knew what lay behind it. Columbus's face was flushed with the effort to contain his anger. He wanted to shout; instead, he slammed his fist on the table, scattering some of the papers on it. He bent over to retrieve what had fallen to the floor, then settled back in his chair and stared at Pinzón, unblinking, for a few moments. His face was set in hard lines, the anger in him threatening to break out into words he knew he would bitterly regret later. When he finally spoke, his voice was brittle.

"The log is a . . . formality." Even as he uttered the words, he knew how inadequate they sounded. It was impossible to avoid the hard reality of what he had done, even though he would swear honestly, on a stack of bibles, that he had been constrained to do it under the terrible circumstances in which they found themselves. If only Pinzón would make an effort to understand, to work with him in their common cause, instead of judging and criticizing at every turn!

Pinzón seemed to be enjoying the other's obvious discomfort. "The distances you logged," he went on in a level tone, "were purposely and deliberately altered. That is, the log you showed everyone, the public *log . . . what was it you*

43

called it? Ah, yes, a formality!*" He made no effort to hide the irony in his voice.*

Columbus, in turn, could not hide his distress. They both grasped the enormity of what he had done, the serious breach of what was everywhere regarded as the most fundamental and imperative priority of a captain at sea, the binding obligation to keep an accurate and detailed log, no matter how brief or routine the trip might be. In the mood he was in, Pinzón was sure to report back to the Sovereigns that Columbus had broken the most basic of maritime rules. He seemed aware of his advantage as he relaxed in his chair, ready to enjoy the eruption he knew was building up. That too would be in his report: how Columbus lashed out at anyone who questioned his judgment or contradicted him, unable to control his temper. Columbus did not turn away from the other's stony stare.

"We sailed for thirty-three days, not counting the time spent in the Canaries," Pinzón went on, his aristocratic air reinforcing the condescending tone behind it. "Risky business to hide that log and set up a second one, showing shorter distances!"

Columbus leaped to his feet, toppling the chair behind him. All restraint was abandoned. "Of course it was risky!" he shouted, leaning over the table so that his face almost touched Pinzón's. "All crucial decisions are risky!"

The other looked up boldly. "Risky indeed, keeping two sets of logs!" He watched smugly as Columbus walked to the other end of the cabin, as though to create distance between them and allow him time to regain his composure. When he turned and spoke, it was a harsh whisper. He was making every possible effort to curb his temper.

"You know as well as I do that the men were ready to mutiny. Most of them were sick, depressed, totally overwhelmed and full of wild notions and fears. Nothing but

44

that vast ocean day after day after day . . . hope vanishing with every passing hour. Those who could still carry on their tasks, grumbled all the while. Our supplies were down to nothing. Water was at a premium, the little that was left, carefully rationed. Every day more men were taken ill. They threatened to kill me, you heard them yourself! What was I to tell them, eh? That I had the same doubts and fears? And if that weren't enough, they kept worrying about those westerly winds pushing always in the same direction. They were convinced I couldn't get around them, coming back. I had a mutiny on my hands. So, YES! I took precautions from the outset; I kept a log that showed we'd gone shorter distances. You would have done the same thing, don't deny it!?"

Pinzón shook his head. Columbus felt himself slipping once more into a quarrel.

"No? You would have done something else? I'd like to know what, exactly!" When the other still did not reply, he went on, with an impatient wave of dismissal: "You sit there judging me! What about your *motives,* your *lies,* your deceptions! *I'm sure you have a perfectly good reason ready to give out for having sailed off as you did, without a word, betraying us all, not giving a thought to the men who depend on us to get them back. That breach, to satisfy your private greed, can be justified; but* my *decision, made to save us all, so we could reach our destination, that one was wrong! Is that it?"*

"You stretch my patience, Columbus!" was the angry retort, as Pinzón pushed back his chair and stood up, glaring. The two men faced one another where they stood, their bodies taut, as though ready to spring at one another. The quarrel was threatening to turn into a fight. Columbus realized that he was itching for one. Pinzón too seemed ready to come to blows. It was grist to his mill. For by now Pinzón's motives had become abundantly clear. His resentment, envy,

and greed were apparent in all that he did and said. He was an opportunist, a man who would stop at nothing to get what he wanted. Columbus no longer could trust him. He knew for certain that unless he could stop him, Pinzón would report back not only the business about the two logs but any and all liberties Columbus had been forced to take along the way to insure their success. Even if he were given a chance to explain his actions, doubts would have been raised in the minds of those who heard such reports. His enemies at Court would renew their attacks; his competence would be questioned; he might even be stripped of his rank of Admiral. All because of Pinzón's envy and greed! It was maddening!

He lowered his gaze, straightened up and sat down again, making a show of examining the maps spread out before him. Pinzón watched him from under hooded eyes for a few seconds, then he too sat down.

It was Columbus who broke the uneasy silence. "Look here, Martín. This journey was like going to the moon! No one could help me track the way, no one can tell me, even now, what we have found, where we are exactly." Pinzón said nothing. Anxious to clear the air, Columbus went on. "Suppose I had turned back when the men began to grumble?" His tone was conciliatory.

Pinzón still had a bone to pick. "You thought you could fool me, keeping that second log?"

"I had no intention of fooling you. I simply was being careful. I would have told you if you hadn't disappeared!"

"I had my reasons. . . ."

"For putting us all in danger? If you hadn't shown up again, we would have been forced back in one ship only, the smallest. The Niña is a good little caravel, but without any back-up?" He let it sink in. Pinzón said nothing. He sat unmoving, staring at the floor.

46

Columbus rose and took from the cupboard behind him two glasses and a small decanter of wine, less than a third full. He cleared a small space on the table for them.

"Let's not quarrel, Martín. All that is behind us. We have proved our instincts were right and have found a new land for our sovereign Queen." As he spoke, he poured a small amount of wine in each glass. When Pinzón did not take the glass offered him, Columbus put it down in front of him, and went on.

"The false log was necessary, and you know it. Those strange winds always blowing in the same direction, forcing us westward, had everyone on edge. And who could have predicted that sea of weeds? The men were frightened to death. You saw it with your own eyes. And every day, more of them coming down with dysentery and other ills. . . . When they started to complain, I knew I had to reassure them somehow. We could not possibly have given up, not then, not with land so near. Yes, I was certain of it! There had to be land close by. Everything pointed to it!"

Pinzon stirred in his chair. He had turned sideways where he sat, his eyes fixed on the cabin door.

"You know as well as I," Columbus resumed, "that, even if we had turned back then, we would never have reached Spain. How could we, without food or water? That too, you know. We had to go on; we had no choice. And it was up to me to find ways of doing that. To avoid a mutiny. Come, Martín, admit it."

Columbus waited for some response. None came.

"Look, all I'm asking is that you consider, for all our sakes, not to mention the second log . . . unless, of course, you are specifically asked about it. But, since we are the only ones who know it exists, that's not likely to happen, is it." He gestured vaguely. "I'm not asking you to go against your conscience; I'm simply asking that you don't make an issue of

47

the two logs. I give you my word, the Queen will be told about them,. . . eventually. . . . "

"Told what?" was the brusque rejoinder, as Pinzon swung back in his chair, to face Columbus.

"Told about the logs, . . . eventually. I will explain everything to her. . . . Listen Martín, faith is not without its moments of doubt, when the devil blasts his way into the soul. But even when I was tortured most by uncertainties and the unexpected, I kept my word, went on. I was true to my commitment. Maybe that's what faith is, just . . . going on and doing what is necessary."

Pinzón laughed. It was not a pleasant sound. "What devil! Sheer stubbornness is more like it. That's precisely when the devil pounces on you, when you talk so insolently about faith and overcoming uncertainties, etcetera, etcetera. You never gave an inch! And you have the nerve to call that faith, . . . commitment! No! You have your own rules. You're right because you say you are!"

"Call it what you like!" answered the other with a frown. "Truth is, I learned a lot from the Portuguese about the currents around Africa, and to the north in that part of the Atlantic. I knew what to expect there. But this wasn't the same. My calculations were correct in one respect. The distances I had worked out were accurate enough. These islands are a sure sign that Asia is close. I'm convinced we're on the right track. Having come this far, are we going to spoil all our plans for the future with these stupid arguments? We're almost there, Martín! My calculations about the width of the ocean were better than Ptolemy's – "

"There!" interrupted the other, slapping his knee for emphasis and looking away, as though addressing a third party. "He's doing it again! What insolence!. . . ." Then, back to Columbus: "You've proved nothing! And Ptolemy can't be dismissed by the likes of you!"

48

Before Columbus's could say anything, Pinzon burst out laughing. "We're a pair of rogues, you and I!" He picked up his glass and held it up in a silent toast. Columbus, visibly relieved, did the same. They drank the meager ration, the dregs of the Admiral's private stock, almost all gone by now, since he had shared it generously with others when rations began to diminish. Even that small residue was an indulgence.

Pinzón put down the glass he had just drained. "All right. I will say nothing about the two logs. . . ."

"Ah!" Columbus could not hide his relief. "We have enough worries!"

Pinzón watched him finish his wine. "I'm sorry about the Santa Maria being wrecked. . . ."

He had scratched a wound that was still hurting. Columbus wondered, even as he felt his blood rise again at the memory, if Pinzón had deliberately brought it up, to make him angry again.

"It's easy to be sorry! Where were you when I needed you? Out there, on your own, looking for gold!"

"You built the fort with the timber that was recovered from the Santa Maria," said Pinzón.

He's relentless, thought Columbus, holding back a curse. Aloud he said: "Do you realize that if you had not returned when you did, we might already have gone, left you behind? What would you have done then, eh? Not that you didn't deserve to be left to the Caribs, but what about the rest of us? We would have had to sail back with one ship only, the Niña! She's a good little caravel and has served us well; but suppose something were to happen on the way back! Without backup the entire enterprise would be in jeopardy. All because of Pinzón's greed!"

"Gold!"

"Greed!"

"Gold! *Isn't that the reason we're here?"* A new confrontation was building up. Columbus turned away abruptly. Pinzón picked up the slack. *"You and your glib talk! Nobody would have listened to you, not for a second, except for the gold you promised would be found in Cathay. You lied when you said the gold was there for the taking!"*

The accusation was unbearable. Columbus turned back and pointed an accusing finger. *"Greed and treachery on your part,"* he shouted, by way of answer.

Pinzón, his head thrust forward, was about to speak, but pulled back instead and laughed again.

"Tell me, Columbus, why can't we have a normal conversation, we two?" The abrupt change in mood again took Columbus by surprise. He shook his head, wearily, as Pinzón went on: *"I just hope you've worked out the magic route that will take us out of here and away from these tropical winds."*

He had hit on just the right note.

"Ah, the return trip. . . ." Columbus relaxed. When he spoke again, his voice was clear and decisive, no residue of anger in his tone. This is where he was most at home. This is what he did best. *"Simple enough, getting back."* He reached for a chart and, as he spoke, traced a line on it with his finger. *"Look here. We work our way north for a while, then northeast, avoiding the tropical winds and steering clear of the weeds. But coming back, Martín, look here, coming back we sail further south and look for the mainland here."* He struck a spot with his finger. Pinzón had come around and stood next to him to see more clearly where he was pointing. *"Then we work our way north again, through the islands, to Hispaniola. From below. By then we will have found – "*

"Never mind the second trip," interrupted the other, waving away what he had just heard. *"Let's think of getting out of here, first. Not having to go through the Carib Islands.*

50

I have nightmares about those cannibals!"

Columbus laughed. "Relax. Let me explain exactly how we do it."

This time Pinzón paid close attention as Columbus traced the steps by which they would reach Spain again.

Chapter Three

RETURN TO SPAIN

They had set sail for Spain in the two remaining ships on Wednesday, January 16, 1493, leaving behind thirty-nine of his men in La Navidad, the fort they had built on Hispaniola from the wreck of the Santa Maria. In the next few days, the Pinta often lagged behind, since her mast was weak and Pinzón had made no effort to repair it before leaving the Indies. They had calm seas and no major difficulties for almost a month.

On February 12, the weather began to change, the seas grew rough. By the next day, the two ships were feeling the strain of high winds and a tempestuous sea. In the storms that followed, the two ships were separated.

On the night of the 16th, Columbus reached an island which he believed was part of the Azores. He was right; they had come to Santa Maria, at that time under Portuguese jurisdiction. Some of the men were taken prisoner. Columbus himself barely escaped capture.

On the 20th, anticipating more trouble, he cut the cables and put out to sea; but more bad weather forced him back two days later. This time the authorities took time to examine the documents Columbus produced. His men were released, and Columbus set sail again for Spain.

In the days that followed, heavy seas,

contrary winds, squalls, and storms battered them. On March 4th, close to the mainland, a terrible gale threatened to wreck the ship. They had reached the rock of Cintra near the river of Lisbon and took refuge there.

From that temporary base, Columbus wrote to the King of Portugal who, wanting to hear all about the adventurous journey, quickly sent for him. He seems to have been treated with courtesy on this occasion; but, the story goes that many at the King's side tried to convince him to have Columbus killed.

On March 13th he set sail for Seville. When he arrived in that city, he discovered that the Court had gone to Barcelona and that Pinzón had survived the storms and had asked the Sovereigns to grant him an audience to bring them news of the journey. It is hard to say what was in Pinzón's mind in making that request, what exactly he said to the Sovereigns in his communication about Columbus and the Niña. The request would have seemed natural enough had he actually seen the Niña go down. He would then certainly have had to report in place of Columbus. Did he really think the Niña had been wrecked in the storms? Whatever was behind his request, he didn't receive the invitation he had anticipated. News that Columbus had made it back safely had already reached the Court. Under the circumstances, Pinzón's request may have aroused suspicions. It is also possible that word had reached the King and Queen of his defection, of how he had gone off on his own and returned only when he found nothing of value to boast about. There had been no word from him for almost three weeks. Columbus was just setting out on the return journey — having given up all hope of seeing Pinzón again in those parts and almost certain that he had preceded him back to Spain in order to get back before him and report to the Court first — when the Pinta reappeared. Pinzón's excuse was that "he was forced to do it" — an explanation that did not go down well with Columbus.

Whatever the circumstances, the Court's response was clear and direct: Pinzón was to wait until Columbus arrived before joining him at Court. Humiliated, he returned to his home in Palos, where he died a short time later.

From Seville, Columbus shrewdly sent a message to the Sovereigns and waited for their reply, instead of continuing directly to Court. Eager to hear about the journey, they invited him to join them in Barcelona — exactly what Columbus wanted. Much better to be invited to the Court than suddenly announce himself — although, under the circumstances, he would have been just as welcome. But this way, the news of his coming would precede him, preparations could be made.

Columbus made the most of his moment of glory. He went in procession through the nearby towns before reaching Barcelona, giving everyone who had gathered along the roads and streets the opportunity to see what he had brought back, especially the Indians in all their glittering ornaments and unusual dress. Animals too were included and exotic birds, including forty colorful parrots. Columbus himself, on horseback, made an imposing figure.

His reception at Court was even more impressive. The Sovereigns received him as though he too were royalty. They stood up to greet him and then invited him to sit down beside them. The commoner from Genoa had been catapulted into fame. The news of his return and all that he had brought back with him spread quickly. At the English Court — Sebastian Cabot later recalled — the event was described as a "thing more divine than human."

The account of his journey, the vivid descriptions of the lovely islands he had discovered and named, the encounters with the native population, the details of all the plants and flowers. and animals they found there, and the prospects for the future, made the reception at Court a truly memorable occasion. Columbus had much to report also about the routes he had established, the new charts and maps that resulted from his careful observations, all the maritime news that he had carefully recorded for so many months. He led forward the Indians he had brought back with him, gave up the gold and pearls he had collected, and spoke of more treasures still to be reaped.

It is hardly surprising that the Indians, the parrots, the gold, and pearls, should have elicited much more interest among the general public and the Court than the extraordinary geographical and maritime observations Columbus had so carefully recorded for so many months. The full implications of what the discovery meant for Europe and the rest of the world were yet to be acknowledged and understood. Nordenskiöld comments in his *Facsimile Atlas* that "scarcely any discovery of importance was ever received with so much indifference, even in circles where sufficient genius and statesmanship ought to have prevailed to appreciate the changes they foreshadowed in the development of the economical and political conditions of mankind."*

The reception at Court was one that would not be forgotten soon. Columbus was provided with quarters in the royal palace and was fêted by all the important families and dignitaries of the city. He had proved his case and now enjoyed the recognition and, yes, the money too, that he had worked so hard for. What more could he ask?

It turned out to be the greatest and — in the large tapestry of his life — the briefest joy he would ever know as Admiral of the Ocean Sea.

FAME AND GLORY!

(Letter to his brother Juonato, from Juan Rodriguez de Fonseca, Archdeacon of Seville.)

May the 19th, Year of our Lord, 1493

My dearest Juonato:

I can't tell you how sorry I was to hear of your indisposition and that you would not be able to join me here

56

at Court to welcome Christopher Columbus, Admiral of the Ocean Sea, back in Spain after his extraordinary voyage.

He has added new honors to his already many accomplishments, all richly deserved, for the journey was an arduous one, full of dangers, but he managed to get back safely, with a minimum loss of men and resources.

He has claimed many new lands in the name of the Spanish Crown and has brought back gold, pearls and other treasures found there. But I leap ahead. Let me tell you first about the reception he received.

When the Admiral learned that the Court was in Barcelona, he chose (correctly, in my opinion) not to proceed there directly but to send a messenger with the news of his return and asked the Sovereigns for instructions. The Queen especially was pleased with the discretion and humility shown in the matter.

You can imagine the excitement at Court and in the rest of the city, when word arrived that Columbus was on his way to meet with the Sovereigns. He arrived on horseback, conspicuous in the long procession that had already passed through many towns. Crowds had followed him along the way and now filled the streets of the city as the procession moved toward the cathedral. There, the bishop offered a mass of thanksgiving and Columbus and his men fulfilled vows they had made while at sea, when the ships were strained to their limit and the men in danger of drowning. No one really believed they would make it. It was indeed a miracle! God's intentions were at work to protect the Admiral and his men.

As they proceeded to the Court, which had been set up in what had been the alcazar of the Moorish kings in the Calle Ancha and was now the residence of the Bishop of Urgil, everyone gaped at the wonders Columbus had brought back, especially at the scantily dressed natives, who made up for the lack of clothing with feathers plumes, ornaments and gold trinkets. The streets overflowed with people. I don't think anyone chose to remain indoors that day. It was an event all of us will long remember!

When they reached the Court, the King and Queen were already there to greet him. They actually rose, and after a while invited the Admiral to sit beside them! Can you imagine that! I couldn't believe my eyes! In the presence of the world, the Sovereigns actually humbled themselves before Columbus!

Many of the cosmographers, dignitaries, and high clergy were there, including the historian Las Casas, who was heard to marvel at the commanding presence of the Admiral. The Sovereigns led the assembled group in prayers of thanks, and the choir of the royal chapel sang the Te Deum.

My dearest brother, I cannot begin to do justice, in these poor words of mine, to the awe and wonder occasioned by the display of birds, plants, gold, pearls and other gifts the Admiral brought back from the new lands. The natives made a special impact there too. At close range, their appearance is uncouth and rough, but some of their ornaments are well made and colorful, suggesting a certain measure of artistic skill. They behave well and seem to respect the Admiral. Oh, and thanks be to God, they had all been converted before leaving the Indies.

I tell, you, Juonato, it was one dazzling display after another. At one point porters came in carrying forty parrots and other birds, all with vivid plumage, also skins of animals not seen before, strange new plants and spices, all sorts of wonderful things. The Queen smiled all the while, quite pleased with it all.

By the way, the brightly-colored parrots, I learned, are sure proof that Columbus has reached India, for the Roman historian Pliny speaks of such birds as indigenous to that part of the world. Marco Polo too is cited as having noted many of the things that Columbus also found. I understand that Peter Martyr is diligently recording the events reported by Columbus, for all posterity to read and study.

Through all this, the Admiral (contrary to the rumors that make him out to be aloof and self-serving) maintained a fine balance of humility and honest pride in his accomplishments. There was nothing disagreeable in his behavior, no arrogance in his speech or manner. He showed extraordinary restraint, especially in the presence of those who initially had placed so many obstacles in his way. Even they have come to respect and admire him.

After his visit at Court (where the Sovereigns had ordered quarters prepared for him during his stay in Barcelona), he was feasted by all kinds of important people. He has been seen riding the streets of the city with the King on one side and Prince Juan on the other. I would not have believed it, but I was told by very reliable sources, who actually saw them together. We were all stunned! It has never happened before, to my knowledge: a commoner riding with the Prince and the King!

I myself attended, the other evening, a banquet given in his honor by Cardinal Mendoza. And just the other day I learned that the Sovereigns will bestow on him a coat of arms on May 20th – although there is some question as to what will be depicted on it. Rumor has it that Columbus has designed it himself – a castle and a lion in the upper section, a group of golden islands in a sea of waves and five anchors in the lower section – but this may not be correct, since the castle and lion are symbols of the royal house and using those symbols for his own blazonry would betray an arrogance not characteristic of Columbus. But, as I said, these are just rumors. Pay no heed to them. There are a few who still would like to find fault with Columbus and take whatever *opportunity presents itself to raise questions and doubts.*

Of course, he has already been amply rewarded with money and titles. He was recently presented with a large gratuity, as well as the reward money that had been promised to whoever first spotted land. They say it was a sailor who first called out the news from his lookout post, but the Admiral was there too and he probably saw it even before the other called out. In any case, Columbus was given that sum too, as well as free lodgings for himself and his followers wherever they go, and the royal seal to be used on letters and orders whenever the occasion presents itself. I was also told (in confidence) that earlier financial arrangements, as well as hereditary rights, have been confirmed and accepted and that many other rewards are in store for him.

It seems that he will stay here until late May, when he returns to Seville to take active part in the preparations for the next voyage to the Indies, scheduled, from what I hear, for later this year.

We are all happy for him, and for ourselves, too, for there is great expectation in the air. India has been reached by a new shorter route, and we are all trembling with excitement at the thought of what this means for Spain.

Meanwhile – and forgive me for closing on such a bleak note – Portugal is rumored to be preparing expeditions of its own and has already approached the Pontiff to set new boundaries to make their explorations and claims legitimate. The Holy Father, you will recall, gave Portugal the patents to sail around Africa. The Portuguese are now asking for access to some part of the newly-discovered lands as well. You must have heard the earlier rumors that they actually tried to kill the Admiral, before he came to Spain with his offer? If the Pontiff does not do something, there may well be bloodshed, especially now that the Portuguese, who (from all I've heard) would not venture out, in spite of having stolen all the notes, maps, and charts Columbus had prepared, are ready to do so now, after Columbus has mapped out the actual routes for the world!

Pray God that these contrary interests do not lead to more bloodshed! The Pontiff will surely resolve the matter, although he has not been predictable in the past and there is some concern as to how he will deal with this matter, when approached, since, although he too is from Aragon, he has shown no particular regard for our King, who rules that land.

I hope, dear Juonato, that I have satisfied in some measure your curiosity about recent events. I will be coming your way shortly and will definitely pay you a visit. Meanwhile, I pray for your speedy recovery.

Your loving brother, Juan

---

*Justin Winsor, *Christopher Columbus* (Connecticut, Longmeadow Press. rpt 1992, p. 248.

Chapter Four

THE SECOND JOURNEY: ACCUSATIONS AND CHARGES

The moment of glory had passed. Even before the celebrations were over, preparations were under way for a second voyage. This time, the Sovereigns understandably were generous. The improbable plan had proved successful and their investment had paid off — to some extent, at least. Much more remained to be done to firm up their claim, and much more remained to be explored and protected. Finding the gold deposits as soon as possible was top priority: it was no secret that Portugal was getting ready to explore the region Columbus had found, eager for a share of whatever it could lay claim to. The Pope had already been approached to establish limits to accommodate both the Spanish and Portuguese claims, and the decision, everyone knew, would be binding. When that happened, Spain would no longer be alone in exploring the Caribbean without restrictions. Columbus had to work as fast as possible and use all the resources at his command in order for Spain to maintain her control of vital areas. The timing was crucial.

He had insisted that it was just a matter of time before he found the major sources of gold and pearls. The stories the Indians told about large deposits of gold further south had convinced him there was much treasure waiting to be reaped. He promised himself and the

Sovereigns he would find it He would bring back more gold and pearls than anyone could possibly hope for. But time was running out. Others might get to the precious mines before they did.

The idea that the land itself might prove to be more precious than gold or pearls was not altogether clear at this point, although, with the founding of Hispaniola, Spain had, in fact, established its first colony.

For the second voyage, Ferdinand and Isabella provided seventeen ships. The fleet included three light speedy vessels expressly built for exploration; a number of cargo ships to carry farm animals, horses, building materials and equipment, everything necessary for a permanent settlement; and ships for at least 1,200 people, the majority of whom were craftsmen, artisans, and simple workmen who would help in the building of the new colony.

What had begun as an uncertain and dangerous undertaking with a small budget but large promises — a shot in the dark, really — was now a top-priority project on the royal agenda. It had gained the focused attention not only of the Sovereigns of Spain but also of the rulers of other major nations of the world. Even though no one still could be sure where Columbus had landed, or that he had really found a shorter route to Cipango and Asia and the sources of rich gold deposits, everyone understood the advantage gained with that first bold voyage, even though many questions still remained.

Spain could not hold back. Not now. It

had led the way, when no one else was ready to do so; it deserved to be the first to reap the rewards. The race was on; others would not be far behind.

Columbus, like everyone else, was aware of the preparations of Portugal, France, and England to follow his tracks. Things would not be easy; but he was ready to do what he did best: explore further and claim larger areas for the Crown. He was ready to assume new tasks as well, in his role as Viceroy of the lands he had discovered. He would have the last word there, also. The difficulties that lay ahead, as governor of Hispaniola, were not yet clear; there were no pressing threats. For now, he could still rely on the wide recognition he had gained and the incontestable power of royal mandates to carry out his new job effectively.

No one disputed his decisions now. Rejected at first by many of the learned experts who had been called to Court to examine his plan, he had become — with the success of the first journey — the uncontested authority in all matters relating to the Indies. He had found — as he had insisted so long he could — a western route to Asia, and in so doing had also laid to rest, once and for all, any lingering doubt that the world, indeed, was round. He had risen to a position of authority and power.

Most important, he had developed a close bond with the Queen. All the while that preparations for the second journey were under way, Isabella sent him frequent reminders about things to be done, specimens to collect and bring back — especially exotic birds and plants. In particular, she exhorted him to make sure the Indians were converted and not abused. At the time, no one could possibly suspect that the treatment of the Indians would become a major issue in the Columbus story, one that would undermine the reputation of the Catholic Sovereigns of Spain and Columbus himself.

Preparations were intense but slow. To help expedite things, the Queen called upon a Florentine merchant living in Seville, Juonato Beradi, to supervise the fitting of the ships. He, in turn, asked another Florentine businessman, Amerigo Vespucci, to help him in the task — the same Vespucci who was soon to play a major role in the age of discovery. His letters about a trip down the eastern coast of Paria, in 1499, would make his name even more famous than that of Columbus.

In Seville, there were always more delays. The Sovereigns themselves were busy writing new orders and issuing last-minute assignments, and commissions. By late June, equipment of all kinds, commodities, and other cargo had been carefully stowed away, including horses, the animals that changed the way of life of the Indians dramatically, for generations to come. By June 30, many of those who would be accompanying Columbus on this second trip had been summoned and told to be ready for imminent sailing. Still, there were delays. The original number of 1,200 passengers had grown and ways had to be found to accommodate the extra passengers. Unlike the meager crew of the first three ships that had hazarded the ocean sea the previous year, the more than 1,200 who sailed out with Columbus on September 25, 1493, included, architects, merchants, scientists, astronomers, government officials, missionaries, horsemen, observers, noblemen, mapmakers, artisans, craftsmen, carpenters, farmers, and just plain ordinary laborers — many of whom would remain in Hispaniola as permanent settlers.

On this second trip, Columbus sailed a more southerly course, avoiding the strange sea covered with weeds. On November 2, noting with his practiced eye the color of the water, and reading correctly the shifting winds, he concluded that land was near. The next day, a Sunday, an island came into view. Columbus named this one, appropriately, Dominica.

His first stop was to be the fort at Navidad, where he had left forty of his men. Along the way, he passed many new islands, to which Columbus gave Spanish names. On November 14, they went by the island Columbus had earlier named Santa Cruz, a place which, he had learned during his first trip, was inhabited by Caribs, who were reportedly cannibals — the most hostile of all the Indians in those parts and the most feared by other Indians. They sailed past and went further on, to Puerto Rico. On November 22, they reached the eastern coast of Hispaniola, where Columbus had left his men. The place appeared deserted. No one rushed forward to greet them. Three days later, a number of decomposed bodies were found. Columbus feared the worst.

A midnight visit to the ships by natives Columbus had befriended on the first trip confirmed his worst suspicions. Navidad had been burned, his men driven into the sea to die or killed while trying to escape. Nothing of the fort remained. Eventually, the details of the massacre surfaced. It was learned that the men had, to a large degree, brought on the disaster themselves by their constant quarreling, their lawless behavior, seeking out and abusing native women, taking from the Indians whatever they wanted, roaming at will to pillage, kill even.

It was a major loss for Columbus, but he could not waste time grieving over it. He had decided, even before sailing back the previous year, that the site of the fort was not a good location for a permanent settlement. Now, he quickly sent out exploratory parties to seek out a new site. None was found in that vicinity and on December 7 he sailed on.

He soon reached what he thought would be an excellent place for a new settlement and gave orders to begin unloading. All goods, equipment, animals — everything the ships had carried — were brought ashore. Building soon got under way. Not long after, all work had to be suspended when the men were debilitated by a mysterious disease the doctors did not recognize and could not cure. It raged its way through the new arrivals, subsiding, finally, when it had run its course. Columbus had encountered what turned out to be malaria.

Building began again. When completed, the new settlement was given the name Isabella, in honor of the Queen.

The quest for gold now began in earnest. Columbus had assured the Sovereigns that the precious metal abounded; that it was simply a question of time before they located the large deposits. All his efforts, however, managed to bring in only a small amount of gold, much less than they had expected and hoped for. Much to his dismay, he discovered — on questioning some Indians — that much of the gold they had collected came not from rich deposits waiting to be tapped but from family treasures handed down as heirlooms, from one generation to another. This was bad news.

On February 2, 1494, twelve of the ships sailed back to Spain with all kinds of specimens and urgent requests for supplies, but very little gold and pearls. It was the beginning of many disappointments for Columbus and for the Sovereigns, but especially for those who had accompanied him in search of easy riches. Their dissatisfaction targeted Columbus, who had promised so much and delivered so little. And when food began to run out and supplies were slow coming in from Spain, the complaints increased. It was Columbus who had brought them to this rude and primitive outpost, a far cry from the splendid lands Marco Polo had described; he was to blame for their difficulties.

The need to plant and till the fields to insure crops the following year had became crucial. The Indians could not share their food indefinitely, as they were asked to do, and in time they too began to grumble. They could not continue to satisfy the inordinate demands made on their supplies. Their own needs were few; their diet a simple one compared to the large appetites of the Spaniards. Their resources were being strained to the limit. In time, the Indians refused to provide any more food or supplies. Their friendliness soon turned bitter.

The emergency this and other difficulties generated forced Columbus to put all his able-bodied people to work. Few relished the idea. Most of them had come to find fortune and new opportunities, not to till the fields or work the mines. The noblemen and other dignitaries who had come on this second voyage objected fiercely to being asked to do menial tasks; not only did they consider it beneath their station to do so but felt it demeaning to work side by side with commoners. To be asked to work at all, in fact, was an insult. In addition, they saw their importance lessened in the light of Columbus's authority and resented having to take orders from him. On their side, the commoners too objected to having to take orders from Columbus, but for a different reason: he was not a member of the ruling elite. Besides, he was a foreigner.

Envy and resentment threatened to destroy all the plans and hopes Columbus had so carefully nurtured. Everyone seemed to have turned against him. His authority began to erode. Matters grew worse as his men became defiant and uncontrollable. Before long, many of them abandoned the colony and disappeared into the forests, taking with them anything they could literally get away with. Like the men left at Navidad, they too roamed together, harassing the natives, stealing their goods and their women, killing at will. They hid well; it was impossible for Columbus to track them down.

To further aggravate an already trying situation, friction developed between Columbus and Bernal Diaz de Pisa, the comptroller assigned by the Crown to audit the colony's books and accounts. When de Pisa insisted on examining those of Columbus, the Admiral was quick to complain at the intrusion into his affairs and made no secret of his indignation. He had nothing to hide but at the same time could not help worrying about what stories de Pisa and others might be circulating about him and what might reach the ears of the King and Queen. At this distance, he could not effectively answer those who might be discrediting him.

As though all of this were not enough to occupy his mind and energies, Columbus had to find ways to fix his ships, which had not been built according to specifications. Leakage and water damage had first developed on the trip over. Among other things, provisions had been spoiled. Obviously the jobbers had trimmed on what contracts had called for, buying inferior materials for less and keeping the difference for themselves. The ships that had sailed back had had to be repaired. Those that remained would need much work before they could be taken out. These setbacks taxed the Admiral's resources as well as his patience.

Still, he had been charged to explore, as

well as govern, and he proposed to do so. He sailed around Jamaica and Cuba, taking careful notes, as always, and recording as many details as possible. Nowhere could he find clear indications of the mainland. When he returned to Isabella on September 29, 1494, he was ill and debilitated. He was carried ashore, his legs too weak for him to walk. To his surprise and joy, he found his brother Bartholomew waiting for him. It was an emotional reunion. The two brothers, always close, had not seen one another for some time. Bartholomew was the best medicine Columbus could have hoped for. He brought welcome news of Columbus's friends, his children and other family members.

There was relief too at having someone with him he could trust implicitly, confide in. Bartholomew was efficient and level-headed, not given to sudden bursts of anger, as his brother often was. His presence seemed to revive Columbus, who soon entrusted him with some of his responsibilities. His presence relieved Columbus of many burdens that had begun to weigh heavily on him.

But in Spain, all sorts of complaints about the Admiral had reached the ears of the King and Queen. Columbus decided it would be prudent to sail back and answer whatever accusations had been made against him. He knew he could explain them away honestly. True, his temper often got in the way, but that was something else. He was innocent of any wrong-doing. He must convince the Sovereigns of that.

PRIVATE AUDIENCE
WITH THE QUEEN

All through the trip back, he had rehearsed what he would say to the Sovereigns and their ministers. If only he knew what had been said about him, if they were actually contemplating charges against him!

On landing, he quickly sent a message to the Court, asking for an audience. The reply came soon enough. The Sovereigns had graciously consented to meet with him.

That morning, he had dressed discreetly. He wore none of his medals. His face was still drawn from the recent illness, but the tired lines in his face spoke of other concerns as well. He seemed to have aged ten years. Now, waiting to be ushered into the presence of the Sovereigns and their cabinet, he cleared his mind and heart, murmured a prayer.

The wait was a short one. He hoped the meeting would also be short; he did not feel up to long arguments. Still, he would take as long as necessary to say what needed to be said. He must be sure the Sovereigns understood his predicament, the immense difficulties they faced in the rough conditions they had been forced to live in. He would explain how the friendly relationship he had established with the natives had eroded because of the lawless actions of defectors. He would tell the King and Queen how he had taken time, notwithstanding these difficulties, to further explore the area, as they had ordered him to do. They would see that he was doing his best to accomplish everything they expected of him.

He followed the guards along corridors he did not recognize, into a part of the palace he had never been to before. These were not the public rooms. Where were they taking him? They paused in front of a beautifully sculptured oak door, which depicted scenes from the Bible. He mouthed a silent prayer.

To his great surprise, he found himself in what was obviously one of the Queen's private rooms. Isabella was sitting; but as the doors closed behind Columbus, she rose and came forward to greet him. Columbus bowed low over the hand she held out to him. He barely had time to adjust to this unusual situation, when the Queen spoke.

"As you see, Columbus, we are quite alone. No need for formalities." She had returned to her chair and motioned Columbus to sit facing her. Columbus did so, his mind racing. What did she mean, "no formalities"? He was momentarily disoriented, trying to grasp the implications of this setting, this one-on-one meeting. Where were the others, where was the King? Was their being alone a good sign or a bad one? Unable to bear the suspense, he plunged in:

"I thank Your Majesty for giving me this audience. What has happened has brought me to the edge of despair. I've done nothing to undermine the interests of the Crown, but there are many who, for reasons we all know, want to blacken my name. God knows I am not without faults, but the insults and charges I have had to bear – " He stopped abruptly, as she held up her hand, interrupting.

"I am sure, Admiral, there has been a great deal of misunderstanding. If anyone has maligned you, I will punish him. You may speak freely with me, before we meet with the rest of the Court." Filled with relief at her words, Columbus burst forth, unable to contain himself:

"It is enough, Your Majesty, that you still believe in me!"

"But I must warn you, Admiral, there is much talk that you kept gold for yourself, that you sent Indians back to Spain to be sold as slaves because you have nothing else to show for your journey. . . ."

"Lies! I kept back as much gold as I needed to reassure the men they would be paid. As for myself, I kept *only what Your Majesty's generosity had established as my share. As for the Indians, they can't be held in captivity, they die if forced to work under our conditions. My plan was, still is, to convert them to Christianity, according to Your Majesty's wishes." There was some truth in what he said about the Indians: for whatever reason, they did not last long if put to hard labor. But there were other tasks they could do, and there were plenty of wealthy people ready to take them into their houses as exotic specimens. . . .*

They both knew he was avoiding a direct answer.

"The gold promised was supposed to be more than what you actually sent back," the Queen went on, skirting the other issue.

"I explained in the letters I sent you, we haven't found the major sources yet. The Indians keep talking about Cibao, further south — "

"That's part of the problem, you see," The Queen interrupted. "Some say you will never find any large deposits."

Columbus leaned forward, as though to make sure she heard him. "The islands I have found are not India, not Asia. I've explained all that to Your Highness. They are rude and primitive outposts. Once we reach the mainland and explore it, we will find everything we have been seeking. There have been so many unexpected difficulties!" He paused to regain his breath.

Isabella sighed. "Seventeen ships, Columbus! Two journeys and seventeen new ships! And still no sign of the treasures of India and China."

Columbus sat back in his chair. He had to find a way to make her understand! God had given him this golden opportunity. . . .

He began again. "Your Majesty, I am certain that I have found the way! I should have stayed on, continue to

74

explore. . . . Perhaps by now I would have found the mainland. . . . But, as you see, I decided to interrupt my activities to report back to you personally, to clear myself with Your Majesty . . . and to request fresh ships and supplies for s third voyage."

The Queen shook her head emphatically. "Not before all this is settled to everyone's satisfaction! I will not have it said – "

Columbus jumped up from his chair. "To everyone's satisfaction!"

The Queen was startled but chose not to comment on the breach of protocol. She had, after all, invited him to a private, informal audience, where she could choose to ignore such an outburst. . . . Out loud, she said:

"The King's, surely!"

Still standing, trying desperately to control his frustration, Columbus went on, his voice low, his words spaced out for deliberate emphasis.

"Those who have slandered me will never *be satisfied! Your Majesty must believe what I say. Beyond the islands, India waits. Marco Polo speaks of islands east of India. I just never thought there were so many! And the fortress destroyed! The Caribs slaughtered my men! . . . . It hasn't been easy!"*

Was he rambling? He sat down again quickly, grateful for the Queen's discretion, for she had let him finish before speaking and did not chide him for interrupting her. But, in her own way, she too was determined to make her point.

"They say, Columbus, that you are the only one who has gained from these trips, that you hold back gold and pearls, that you have hidden away a large store of precious things for your own profit."

"God is my witness!" he cried out, gripping the arms

75

of his chair, so that he wouldn't jump out of it again, "I have forced my men to give up every piece of gold, every pearl found or gotten by trade. Everything is kept in a large hold, each piece carefully marked and labeled as to weight, size, appearance, who brought it in, where it came from – "

Isabella interrupted, raising her voice to reach over his: "Then, Admiral, there is the matter of the fort!"

Columbus chose his words carefully. "Navidad was destroyed by hostile Indians, Caribs, while I was here in Spain. But even it I had been there, with my men, I could not have saved them or myself or the fort. We were betrayed!"

He watched for some reaction. The Queen sighed. "Still, it is difficult to explain all this to the satisfaction of others!" Her words, like an arrow that had finally hit its mark, cut through the air and stabbed his fragile composure. He managed to remain seated, but his anger could not be wholly contained. He brought his closed fist down hard on the small table beside him and glared at the Queen.

"Satisfaction of others??!!" he shouted. Isabella stared back at him. Columbus quickly knelt before her, his despair evident in his every move. Abruptly, he covered his face with his hands. When he spoke again, it was a mere whisper.

"Forgive me, Your Majesty." He hazarded to look up at her. "I don't know where to turn! If you don't believe me, who will?!"

The Queen watched him in silence, then motioned him back into his seat.

"Yes, you have made enemies, Columbus. All great men do. There are many out there who would like to replace you. I know all that. But I said I would protect you, didn't I?" She reached across and touched his arm lightly. "You must confide in me, Columbus," she went on gently; "how else can I plead your cause!"

Relief flooded over him. It was the first explicit indication that she was still prepared to defend him.

"I am a simple man, Your Majesty. The sea is my home. I am not at ease in palaces," he went on, with a wide sweep of his arm, "among crowds, with men in high places waiting for me to contradict myself – "

The Queen cut him off. "I will tell you bluntly that the King is not pleased. It has taken me much effort to convince him that he has no grounds to suspect you, no reason for displeasure, that you have done your duty honestly and have not betrayed our trust." She paused, then rose from her chair and took a few steps away from where Columbus had also risen and stood watching her. She turned to face him, and went on.

"When your friend Pinzón –"

" – No friend of mine!

" – sent me that incredible letter, assuming you had been drowned at sea, the Niña lost in the storms off the coast, when he asked to be received to take credit for your discoveries – "

"He wished me dead!"

" – I did not hesitate for a moment, did I? I cut him off, as I would cut off a traitor. I told him I could never again trust him and had no wish to ever see him again. . . ." She paused.

"Yes, but . . . now?"

She returned to her seat and motioned Columbus to resume his.

"Columbus, when everyone else was saying you were mad, when my counselors were telling me that you spoke sacrilege and that your plan was impossible, demonic even, when my own beloved King spoke harshly on the matter, I trusted you and backed you. . . . I remind you of this, Columbus, so that you may gain new confidence and trust in

77

me still. . . . . I have other reasons for wanting this expedition to continue, and those are clear enough, I think." She had been resting her head on the cushioned back of her chair, her eyes closed. Now she sat up and met the Admiral's gaze.

"Columbus, we are alone here. I made a point of meeting you privately, so you could say what you wish. It is the only opportunity we will have to speak openly to one another. Out there, the world is ready to destroy you! I know all that." She gave him a sad smile. "So, let's get on with it! Get it all out, so we can move on!"

She assumed a businesslike air. "There has been a lot of talk about your finding some God-forsaken place, not India." Columbus leaned forward as though to speak. "I know, I know, you explained all that, but let me finish. They say the natives there have nothing in common with the Indians we are familiar with. They insist that there is little gold in the islands where you have landed, that it comes from some other place, further south or perhaps further west. . . . They say that there is no sign of civilization in those islands, that some natives are cannibals in fact, and that there are no rajahs, no kings, no castles. That the whole area is untamed, full of trees and forests. That the natives are primitive and uncouth." She paused, waiting for him to absorb it all. "That's what they say, Columbus!"

Suddenly, he was galvanized into motion. He rose, unable to hide his excitement.

"India is just beyond, Your Majesty! You must believe me! Just beyond, to the west, beyond Hispaniola, beyond the other islands, or perhaps to the southwest. That's my plan! To go further south, further west, on the next trip and reach the mainland from below."

The Queen frowned. "Surely, India would not be that far south!"

"I thought so, too," he replied confidently, "but the

78

maps we have may be wrong –"

"And . . . if nothing is there?"

*For a moment he stared at her, uncomprehendingly.
"No, no, what do you mean 'nothing'? The Indians all speak
of other great areas, the gold, the pearls, all come from
further south or southwest!"*

*The Queen rose. Columbus did the same. She held
out her hand. "Let's make a pact. We'll worry only about
what is in our control. Agreed?" She waited for Columbus to
take her hand and bow over it. "The future will unfold, soon
enough, full of surprises!"*

*"Pinzón may have been right, after all! He said I
was . . . stubborn!"*

*"Perhaps you are, but your success gives him the
lie!" were her parting words.*

*"I will find India! Yes, I am stubborn enough for
that!" he whispered as he was escorted from the room.*

*Back in his quarters, he paced nervously, muttering
to himself. The audience had gone well, all things considered,
but he was still on edge, still under the strain of the ordeal he
had suffered. Oh, God! Had he really interrupted the Queen?
Shouted at her? He shook his head violently at the outrage he
realized he had committed. Thank God, no one else was
present to hear him! The Queen, bless her, must have realized
what he was going through. She had not even scolded him!*

*He lay down on the bed and closed his eyes; trying
to relax. Instead, anxiety crowded his consciousness. . . .*

*All the money and time and men and hardships –
for what? To be brought up on charges of theft! God help us!
Surely the Queen understands my responsibilities to my
brothers, my sons – what's wrong with that? Why should I
feel guilty about taking care of my own? Why do I feel guilty
even when I don't know why or about what?*

There would be no further talk of charges, but he

79

was still upset and nervous about the implications those accusations had raised. He had done nothing wrong, by God! Nothing he could not justify. Nothing that was not right and proper. What he had taken was due him, all part of the agreements set up before the first journey and other arrangements made since then. It was that rascal Pinzón who had first started the rumors and accusations, turning the men against him back then, even before they landed. He had been a thorn in his side from the beginning. Well, he had gotten what he deserved! The Queen had refused to see him! Imagine! The scoundrel thought he could claim for himself the honors and rewards that rightfully belonged to him, to Christopher Columbus! Even if the Niña had indeed been wrecked in the storms that hit the coast and everyone on board had been drowned, those honors belonged to his heirs, to his sons Diego and Fernando, his brothers, his uncles. . . .

He drifted off into an uneasy sleep. Suddenly Pinzón was at the foot of the bed, laughing.

"You gave her a hard time, back there! She could have had you arrested!"

"Ah, the devious one, Even dead, he manages to get around! So you found your way in to listen. Yes, you always enjoyed watching others squirm. Always ready to put others down. Well, since you were there, you heard what she said about you!"

"I'm not concerned with that. What I did served a purpose. I was your conscience, your demonic side if you prefer. We all have one, you know."

"I trusted you, damn it! And you were tempted, like all the others. You might still be working against me if you hadn't —"

"Hadn't died? You're probably right. . . . Gold was the great temptation. Always is. Not just for me. Even you were tempted, are you going to deny it? We're all human,

Columbus. All subject to temptation."

"Have you come all this way to remind me of that?"

"In part, yes. But also to give you some advice."

"Ah, that's more like it! And what great insight are you so anxious to share with me?"

"Don't count on anyone, my friend!"

"Not even the Queen?"

"Fame, wealth, promises, make a man vulnerable. No, not even the Queen!"

"You doubt the sovereign Queen? She would never betray me! But you wouldn't know anything about that, about trust and loyalty! The Queen will never betray me!"

"That's not what I said. . . . But, no, not the Queen. HISTORY! History betrays us all. . . . Did you know that Marco Polo was actually taken prisoner in a sea battle and thrown into jail in your own Genoa? Marco Polo in a Genovese jail —"

" — I know that — "

" — where he wrote, no, where he dictated — never did learn to write — where he dictated his account of the journey into China. Imagine!"

"Even Marco Polo speaks of the islands near India, the islands I have found — "

"Oh, you'll find many islands, Columbus. But the Queen — "

" — The Queen? The Queen made very clear that I had done an incredible thing!"

"Who ever said you had done less?"

"India is my life, my glory! Who else would have dared what I dared, eh? I dared! Without thinking of all the problems in store for me, not lingering on the fears and uncertainties. Even you would not have had the guts to go out there on your own. Admit it. You came because of me, because you knew I had worked it all out. I found land

81

exactly where I had said we would. And yet, in some demonic way, you had hoped for me to be proved wrong! Oh, I could feel it, your resentment, your envy. It was so palpable, at times I could feel it cutting into me, like the blade of a knife! And even though we would all have been lost if we had not found land when we did and you would not have had an opportunity to tell the world what an incompetent fool I was, you still hoped for the worst! Just waiting for something to go wrong. Are you going to deny it?"

He woke up with a start. For a moment he was disoriented at finding himself in the unfamiliar room. He shook his head, as though dislodging the dream that had invaded his uneasy sleep.

There was still much to do before leaving Spain, but the most important thing was that the Sovereigns – thank God! – were ready for a third voyage. He prayed that the new agreements that had to be prepared and signed before he sailed back to Hispaniola would not take too long. He was anxious to get back, to sail again, to find the strait that would take him into Indian waters.

He rose from the bed to draft letters he was planning to send to Hispaniola with the ships that he would be sending back directly, while he went exploring. The dream, so vivid and distressing at the time, was soon forgotten.

Chapter Five

THE THIRD JOURNEY:
PEARLS, GOLD, AND INDIANS

The King and Queen had provided six new ships and fresh provisions for his third voyage. He headed back from Spain with his small fleet on May 30, 1498. After a brief stop at the Canaries, he sent three of his ships, with urgent and long-awaited supplies, directly on to Santo Domingo, the new site his brother Bartholomew had built in his absence on the southern coast of the island, where rich gold mines had been found. With the other three ships, Columbus resumed his explorations.

His only goal now was to find the strait that would take him into the Bay of Bengal and, just beyond, India.

The heat was unbearable as they reached the Equator. Wine and water casks burst; the men suffered and were afraid the heat would destroy the ships as well, but after a few days the air cooled, and, as conditions improved, the men were reassured. On July 31, he reached the mouth of the great river Orinoco. There the natives shot arrows at them. Columbus noted that these particular Indians also used shields to protect themselves — the first time he had seen the natives wear armor of any kind. He decided not to linger or try pacifying them with gifts but sailed right on.

Near the mouth of the Orinoco, he discovered a strait. It was the first of many moments that were to raise his hopes only to have them shattered almost immediately.

He was amazed at the huge billows that rolled from the river into the ocean and dismayed to find the passage through the strait the most dangerous he had ever encountered. Strange currents and unusual tidal movements kept pushing the ships back. With tremendous effort, he finally managed to bring the vessels into the body of water that lay beyond, only to discover he had entered a gulf and that he had discovered another island — a large one this time, but an island nonetheless.

Columbus called the southern strait The Serpent's Mouth and, the even more hazardous one at the northern end, The Dragon's Mouth. Because of the three peaks that dominated it, he named the island Trinidad, but he may also have wanted to pay tribute to the Holy Trinty.

While sailing north on the western side of the gulf, he discovered the water was fresh and drinkable because of the many rivers that emptied into it. There he met friendly Indians, who referred to the place as Paria and provided Columbus with fresh provisions and something that could have passed as wine. A considerable amount of gold was collected as well as pearls which, the Indians told him, came from a nearby fishery, to which they directed him. There Columbus collected a large number of the pearls and, before leaving, instructed the friendly natives to collect and put aside for him as many more as they could find: he would return later to claim them. The Indians agreed.

It was probably here, on the western coast of what the Indians called Paria, across from Trinidad, that Columbus first set foot on the southern part of great continent which, according to all known records, neither he nor any other European yet knew existed.

Earlier, in a letter to the Queen, he had compared Hispaniola to the Mount Sopora of Solomon. The beauty of the places he now visited — their lush vegetation, the mild weather, all the other attractive features he observed — fed what was to become an obsession: he was convinced he had found the Earthly Paradise described in the Bible. The fresh waters that sweetened the gulf through which he had sailed flowed, he believed, from the fountains of Eden down the slopes of the beautiful terrain they saw before them. Other similar comparisons appear frequently in his writings at this time. He also recalls stories from the Middle Ages, which pointed to the East as the seat of Paradise. He had proved the earth was round but suddenly began to wonder if it might not be pear-shaped instead. The forces that had steered them to the top of the gulf strongly suggested a narrowing which brought them, he believed to where the earthly paradise was located. These extravagant imaginings might have continued, had he not been forced back to Hispaniola.

He had been absent from the colony for two years. The men had grown restless, supplies were dwindling, the ships needed repairs; many of the provisions they were carrying had spoiled. There was no choice: he knew he had to head back. as soon as possible.

The route he chose was guesswork at best. They had gone much further south than ever before, in unfamiliar waters, and the tropical winds often blew them off course. Besides, not even the Admiral knew where Santo Domingo, the new capital, was located; he had not been there yet.

But, as so often in the past, Columbus's navigational skills got them through. On August 19, 1498, the island came into view and a ship approached. It was Bartholomew, the Admiral's brother, come to lead them into the harbor of Santo Domingo.

Columbus had made it back safely, and with more gold and pearls than he had ever gathered before. On both counts, he had every reason to be pleased — not to mention his miraculous discovery of the Garden of Eden!

The real miracle was his having set foot on a huge continent unknown to the ancient Greeks and all who came after, including the cartographers, astronomers; and scientists of Columbus's day: a land mass that extended from the northernmost regions to far below the equator in the south. Paradoxically, even though he never realized what he had found, it was his bold venture that took away the old fears of the Atlantic as an unknown quantity and made other explorers follow in his wake and eventually reach a very different conclusion about the new lands in the west.

For more than a year, rumors had been circulating about land in the northern regions.

John Cabot, a Venetian merchant and, like Columbus, Genovese by birth, had settled in Bristol, England and in 1496 had approached King Henry VII for patents to explore the waters in the north. The King had granted him permission in March of 1497, and two months later Cabot left Bristol and sailed west to see what he could find in that direction. He landed at Cape Breton on June 24, or, as some would have it, on Labrador or Newfoundland, and claimed the territory for England. Like Columbus, he thought he was in the vicinity of Asia — perhaps on the mainland itself.

The claim was immediately contested by Spain, but without success. In the end, England won out. Further south, Portugal would also succeed in her claims and would emerge as a formidable competitor. While Columbus was still trying to find the elusive passage into the Indian Ocean, Vasco da Gama sailed down the length of western Africa, the year before Columbus's third journey, rounded the Cape, and reached India on the other side. Two years later, in 1499, men like Amerigo Vespucci and Pedro Alvarez Cabral would insure for Portugal important and lasting acquisitions in the new lands. But in 1498, Spain still retained an advantage as the major player in the Caribbean.

On August 30, 1498, Columbus landed for the first time in Santo Domingo, the new capital his brother had established, where rich deposits of gold had been found. He planned to stop there only for so long as it took to send news to the Queen about the new sources of pearls and gold. Then he would leave the island in his brother's care again and, with fresh supplies and several of the fastest caravels available, pick up the pearls the Indians in Paria were holding for him and. sail from there directly to Spain.

Fate decided otherwise. His careful plans were about to crumble.

A LETTER TO THE QUEEN

Isabella had been pleased with much of the news from Columbus. She had retreated to her private chambers to read his letter when it had first arrived. She had already shared it with her husband and would share it with her counselors the next day, but at the moment she was intent on reading it again, this time out loud, for the benefit of one of her ladies-in-waiting, a close friend and distant relative, whose nephew had gone with Columbus on the second trip and was still in Hispaniola.

"'From the Canaries, I sent three of the ships directly to the new colony, with supplies and instructions. With the other three ships I followed a route parallel to the western coast of Africa, down to the Cape Verde Islands.'"

Her friend frowned. "Good Lord, that far down?" The Queen shrugged off the question and resumed:

"'Then a more westerly course, still going south, further south than anyone has gone before . . . then gently westward again. We came to another island, but this one was strange.' . . . "

The other interrupted. "What does he mean by strange?" The Queen held up a restraining hand by way of answer.

"'Three peaks, the first land since the Cape Verde Islands. I called the place Trinidad. . . . And two openings

on the western side, so, yes, Trinidad was another island, a large one, and very lovely, but, still, only an island. . . . My biggest surprise was to find that the water there was fresh. The men drank their fill. But we were almost shipwrecked trying to get through the straits at both ends! The unusual currents, just below the first opening, made the passage into the gulf most difficult. A superhuman force seemed to be pushing us back as though to keep us from getting into the waters beyond. At the northern end, an even greater force – if that's possible – swept us out into the sea. Both times, I feared for our lives, but we came through without any serious damage, thanks be to God! I called the opening we came through from the south The Serpent's Mouth, and the one at the northern end The Dragon's Mouth.'"

"Lord have mercy!" the Queen's friend exclaimed.

The Queen nodded and went on: "'The fresh water suggests a great inland river, but it must be tremendous to cascade into the sea with such force. . . . Indians there too, with more pearls than you can imagine, and they claimed to have gotten them from that body of water. Pearls and gold, more than I have seen in any other place, some of it worked with remarkable skill.

"'We sailed north along the coast, past any number of islands, then westward as the land turned sharply in that direction. But the men began to grumble. We didn't know exactly where we were, except that Hispaniola lay to the north. I took a course northwest by north but had to make adjustments along the way, partly because of the winds that kept blowing to the west and also because of unpredictable currents and the possibility of reefs. Still, my calculations proved correct, and we saw Hispaniola once again.

"'There, to my great consternation, I found much turmoil. The rebels have grown even more intractable and defiant under their leader, Francisco Roldán, a man I

89

thought I could trust and to whom I gave the title of Chief Magistrate before leaving for Spain. What irony! He was to mete out justice, instead he has become the chief instrument of injustice, opposing the authority which Your Majesty entrusted to me, opposing me at every turn – insisting, all the while that he has not disobeyed Your Majesty but is simply demonstrating against my self-serving ways. He has drawn many Chiefs into a conspiracy against me, urging them to complain about my handling of things. As a result, nothing is being mined, nothing is being grown. I may have to resort to extreme measures, if an agreement is not reached soon.

"'I sincerely hope Your Majesty will protect me against the accusations these cruel and debauched men have raised in order to satisfy their own lusts and cupidity. They have proved hard taskmasters with respect to the Indians, doing with them what they please. The climate and conditions here have not helped any. There is much sickness, not all of which is treatable, the doctors have told me.

"'In spite of everything, I have carried on my work to the best of my ability, mindful of Your Majesty's instructions.

"'I pray this finds you in good health and that the pearls and gold I have sent have arrived safely.

Christopher Columbus
Admiral of the Fleet of the Ocean.'"

Isabella put the letter to one side and closed her eyes. Her friend watched her in silence. She knew how much the mistreatment of the Indians pained the Queen, how again and again she had exhorted Columbus not to sell them into slavery. . . .

She also knew that he had disobeyed her orders, that Indians were being forced to work the plantations and the mines. It had been a desperate measure, he had insisted. The

90

orders he had issued, calling on the entire colony to take on essential tasks, were brazenly rejected or ignored. His men had rebelled; the privileged hildagos had objected even more strenuously: in no way could they be expected to work alongside commoners!

Columbus had had no choice but to put the Indians to work. It had been a terrible decision and most unChristian. In the end, it had not worked out at all. And now there were these current reports of growing unrest. The Queen, everyone knew, was having a hard time convincing the King they should not listen to the rumors about Columbus losing control of things and the stories that were circulating about his keeping large stores of gold and other treasures for himself. This letter would surely add fuel to the tensions at Court, raise more questions about the Admiral's ability to rule the colony. Earlier, the Queen had confided to her friend that she was not altogether sure she could stem the bitter animosity generated by the accusations of his enemies. There was serious talk of bringing him back to stand trial –.

The Queen took a deep breath, a heavy sigh really, and opened her eyes. She gripped the arms of her chair to pull herself up. When she spoke, it was barely a whisper. Her friend could hardly make out the words, as she hastened to follow the Queen from the room.

"Dear Columbus," she said to no one in particular, "what have we gotten ourselves into!"

Chapter Six

NEW CHARGES:
COLUMBUS IN CHAINS

In Santo Domingo, Columbus realized he could not leave for Spain as planned. His two-year absence had seriously eroded his authority. Earlier hostility had escalated to open rebellion, which had quickly spread to other outposts and was now almost impossible to control. While he was away, many more men had defected for an easy life of license and lawlessness.

The good news was that the Sovereigns had confirmed Bartholomew in his new title of Adelantado, his authority as governor, when Columbus was absent, not to be questioned. Columbus himself had had some of his titles reinstated and certain sums restored, according to earlier agreements, which at one point had been revoked and his share of the wealth reduced in the light of growing expectations and new exigencies.

These good tidings were obscured, however, by news of increasing defections and of an alliance the rebels had succeeded in making with several Indian tribes, who had become more and more hostile because of the inordinate demands made on them by the administration. To restore some semblance of authority in the face of growing opposition, Bartholomew had meted out cruel punishments. He had hoped, by showing a strong hand, to quell insurrections and lessen tensions.

His actions, meant to bring an end to the troubles, proved disastrous instead.

One reason for the growing opposition was the antagonism generated by the refusal of the Adelantado to allow workers to share in the profits from the gold mined near the Haina River, on the southern coast of the island, where rich deposits had been uncovered and where the capital had been moved in order to facilitate mining operations. Both Columbus and his brother Bartholomew (who had been left in charge while Columbus went exploring) were accused of hoarding treasure for themselves and not allowing others to reap some gain from their hard work. Many also charged Columbus with dereliction of duty, accusing him of having abandoned the colony to Bartholomew's harsh rule. When Columbus returned, after his two-year absence, the situation had deteriorated even further. Opposition to the administration was widespread.

The blueprint for a more regulated and permanent form of government that would bring peace and prosperity to Santo Domingo obviously was not working. The hildagos had made clear, from the beginning, when scarcity of laborers and animals had forced Columbus to put everyone to work, that they resented such an order. They had sailed with Columbus to find gold, not to be used as menial laborers, alongside ordinary commoners.

The Indians too had strongly objected when ordered to produce large quantities of food and essentials to help feed the Spanish colony. It was a burden they could not possibly carry. The Spaniards required a much more plentiful supply of food than the Indians, who lived on a small diet. The maize and the other staples the natives grew were barely enough for their meager needs; they could never produce the quantities needed to satisfy the large appetites of the Spaniards or to supplement the poor yield of the new plantations, which had to produce enough to feed the more than 1,200 new colonists who had arrived with Columbus on his second voyage. Even had they wanted to, the Indians could not have met such demands.

To avoid being captured and punished for their disobedience, the Indians had made a drastic decision: they burned their villages, before the Spaniards could get to them, and fled into the hills. Columbus had acted quickly, hoping that a show of strength and authority would bring the renegade Indians around: he hunted them down and killed many of them. Instead of bowing to this show of power, the Indians who survived grew even more fierce in their determination to fight the Spaniards in every possible way.

As conditions became more desperate, Columbus found his control over the colony threatened with each passing day. The Indians had become his enemies; the men still in the colony had grown more aggressive in their lawless behavior. The governor's power was resented; his authority openly challenged with impunity. When a conspiracy was uncovered, those in power quickly hunted down the leaders and hanged one of them. This action served only to exacerbate an already tense situation. Eventually things came to a head and sparked an open rebellion, led by Francisco Roldán, the former mayor of Isabella.

All this had happened in 1494. When Columbus arrived to Santo Domingo in August 1498, he found that Roldán was still in Yaragua, where he had fled two years earlier. He had taken with him most of the able-bodied men in Isabella.

Back in his role as governor of the island, Columbus realized that he must reach some kind of agreement with Roldán but found it extremely difficult to approach him or lure him to a meeting. He persisted, however, and in due course succeeded in getting Roldán to enter into negotiations that would bring back all the defectors and restore peace, as well as a much-needed work force, to the colony.

Roldán — a precursor of the tough union leader of our time — insisted on extraordinary conditions and demands. With great misgivings, Columbus agreed to all of the rebel leader's terms. These included back payment to all his men for two years of labor, even though they had not done a single day's work all the time they had been in hiding. Roldán himself asked for and was given the title of *alcalde mayor*, high mayor of the entire island.

When the ratifying of the terms agreed on took more time than anticipated, Roldán boldly used the delay as an excuse to make further demands. This time he asked that each

95

of his men also receive land as well as a number of Indians to work it. The agreement was finally ratified and signed. The only condition Roldán would accept was that the Indians be instructed in the rudiments of the Christian faith.

For Columbus, it amounted to a public humiliation; the fallout from it would nearly destroy him. On the other side, Roldán and his men rejoiced: they had won a major victory and made the most of it.

None of the players in this drama could possibly predict the lasting consequences of such a reconciliation.

On the positive side, the peace terms mark a turning point in the history of the growing colony, signaled by a number of dramatic socio-political-economic changes. The seeds for a more representative government had been sown. Men of low rank had been turned into landowners and masters of a large work force. Most important: with their new status, these men now had an effective voice in the government of the colony and could take part in all the important decision-making.

On the negative side, the terms of the agreements eroded the authority of Columbus still further and also incurred the displeasure of the Sovereigns, the Queen especially. The large concessions he had made in order to insure peace in the colony had also further alienated the hildagos, who saw the rebels, now rich property owners, as a threat to their superior status. They stood rank together in accusing Columbus of demeaning the nobility and allowing riffraff to become wealthy at their expense, even to have a place and a voice in the government.

Seemingly reconciled to the authority of Columbus as the Crown's representative, Roldán, on his part, had managed to have his long-standing complaints against Columbus relayed to the King and Queen. Columbus himself was not aware, until later, of his loss of credit at Court, where reports about his ineffectual rule and his personal priorities and self-interest had found their way.

The Sovereigns felt they could no longer ignore or dismiss the accusations that Columbus was not equipped to administer the growing colony effectively. Besides, the enterprise had gone far beyond the initial fact of discovery. Spain had entered a new phase; its goal was now focused on developing and insuring its claims in the new lands. The situation called for talents and skills which clearly Columbus did not have.

The Crown had also become aware of the alarming conflict that was brewing between commoners, who realized that in the new land they had a chance at riches and honors they never could claim before, and those with rank, who insisted on exercising all their special privileges and resented the claims of upstarts. The Sovereigns decided to take advantage of Roldán's new prominence, and the authority he had gained, to lessen the intense class struggle that had developed. Roldán himself had insisted throughout his campaign against Columbus that his attacks were against the foreigner, the outsider, not against the Crown itself. Roldán's expressed loyalty to the Sovereigns, who had recognized his new status, could prove instrumental in bringing the different groups together in their common national interest.

With this strategy in mind, the King and Queen dismissed Columbus as governor of the colony and named Francesco de Bobadilla in his place.

Bobadilla was a Knight of the Order of Calatrava and quickly grasped the advantage of fueling the national fervor that Roldán had evoked in his insistence that he never meant to undermine the Crown. His assignment, even though temporary (for it was understood that someone else would soon arrive to take on the permanent post), encouraged Bobadilla to follow the policy which the pernicious foreigner, the man he held in contempt, had initiated: he continued to give away land and Indians. His temporary assignment also encouraged him to close his eyes to the arbitrary and self-serving actions of the men who had returned with Roldán. He decided to make no waves and to leave the hard decisions to his successor.

Bobadilla has been described as the most violent, ambitious, and self-serving man ever to set foot in the land Columbus had claimed for Spain. There is no question that he treated Columbus with cruel contempt when he arrived in 1500 to assume his post. He immediately deprived Columbus of all his goods and property and stripped him of his command as well as his honors. As a last expression of haughty arrogance, the new governor ordered that Columbus be taken back to Spain, where he was to answer charges, in chains.

No one came forward to defend him. Bobadilla had shrewdly bought the support of Roldán and his men by allowing them to keep their new wealth and continue the easy life of property owners. He could afford to be generous, knowing that most of the land grants and Indians would eventually revert to the Crown. It wasn't his headache. For now, he could claim to have restored peace, if not law and order in any true sense. Everyone was happy and relaxed. When the moment came to denounce Columbus, no one took exception.

With the arrival of the new governor, Nicolás de Ovando, in July 1502, Bobadilla's lax rule came to an end. Ovando had precise instructions from the Sovereigns about what should come next. They had allowed Bobadilla to have his way during the period of adjustment that followed Roldán's reconciliation; but with Ovando, restraints were restored, the laws applied more rigorously. The Sovereigns, who for a number of reasons had not been pleased with the terms Columbus had accepted from Roldán, wanted Ovando to find ways to override them.

The rebellion and its aftermath guided Ferdinand and Isabella in their instructions to the new governor. Ovando was to establish his authority firmly, not only over the men Roldán had brought back into the colony but also over the 2500 new settlers who had sailed to Santo

Domingo with him. Explicit orders were given to stop the plundering of native villages and the abuse of the Indians; they were not to be used for forced labor or sold as slaves.

It was understood that any agreement reached with Roldán could not be dissolved, or the grants received be taken away from his people without grave consequences. Ovando must find other avenues to obey the orders given him, other ways to correct the errors made by his predecessors. Above all, he had to avoid any new confrontations.

Things were made easier by the fact that Roldán himself and many of his associates had conveniently drowned in a hurricane which overtook the ship in which they were returning to Spain, soon after Ovando's arrival in the colony. Still, the influence he exerted on the rest of his followers had to be destroyed if the colony was to be spared new insurrections.

In a clever maneuver, Ovando saw to it that a good number of Roldán's men married the Indian women with whom they had been living. The rationale for this strategy was clear and unambiguous. Once those relationships were legalized, Ovando could take back the lands and the slaves, since the owners had changed their legal status by marrying Indian women and had no right to those properties.

With the leader of the rebellion and its chief conspirators out of the way, Ovando was able to carry out his plan. But the new governor had his own agenda. It soon became clear that he was not at all prepared to allow the Indians he freed to return to their villages and pick up where they had left off. He explained to the Queen — who had repeated in 1501 that the Indians were not to be mistreated in any way — that without the natives to work the mines and the plantations, the colonists would starve, the colony itself collapse. He made clear that the slave trade was their only possible source of much-needed revenue and that any orders from the Crown, limiting or preventing the use of Indians for forced labor, under the fragile truce that had been reached and at such a distance, were bound to fall on deaf ears. Punishing those who did not obey would cause more disruption. The situation was desperate.

The Queen acquiesced. A plan was quickly drawn up and legalized making all slaveowners responsible for providing a certain number of Indians for work in the mines and on the plantations. Each owner would also be held responsible for teaching his slaves the rudiments of the Catholic faith.

The period of adjustment was over. The colony had entered a new phase. The first exuberant response to the great discovery had turned into the onerous task of insuring the survival of the colony.

One large problem had emerged, even before Ovando took over: getting people to settle in Hispaniola. Even the promise of gold was no longer an enticement to prospective colonists. Those who returned to Spain from Isabella or Santo Domingo were dramatic proof of what they had endured: they came back looking haggard, ravaged by mysterious diseases like malaria. Almost half the original population had died in the colony.

Those returning to Spain also had stories to tell about mismanagement on the part of Columbus and his brother Bartholomew, about the rigorous discipline they had imposed, the hard measures used to insure obedience. Columbus was again accused of greed and of working against the interests of the Crown. It became all too evident that the prejudice against him had not diminished: the people he was given to govern resented having to take orders from a foreigner and a commoner. Combined with those feelings was envy for all the honors he had reaped and the continued support of the Queen. Jealousy and animosity had grown deep roots.

It was clear, under the circumstances, that Columbus could no longer play an effective role in the future of Hispaniola. Meanwhile, the reports that continued to reach Spain brought matters to a head. The Sovereigns realized they must act. Columbus was recalled to Spain.

It was Bobadilla, still in charge, who gave orders that he was to be kept in chains for the duration of the trip, like a common criminal.

LAST ENCOUNTER WITH THE QUEEN

He knew it would not be an easy meeting. This time he had been called, no, ordered, to return, not like the last time, when he had chosen to report to the Queen in person.

In the end, that meeting had turned out well. She had given him six fresh ships and new instructions, which clearly indicated she still trusted him and supported him wholeheartedly. But this time –

Again, she had chosen to see him in her private quarters, where she now paced nervously in front of him. He stood awkwardly, his head down, his eyes lowered, his entire body bent under the weight of her anger.

Clearing his head of the anxious thoughts crowding in on him, he focused his attention on what she was saying.

"Do you realize how much trouble you have caused me? If it were not for my protecting you, your enemies would have you in the dungeons by now and you would soon be forgotten!"

Weariness overcame him. He struggled to get words out. "Your Majesty has always supported me and my good name. . . ."

"To learn from my own husband that you defied our orders!"

Lack of sleep and worries had kept him awake all night. Weariness threatened to overcome him where he stood. He swayed for a moment but quickly recovered. Habit cautioned him to avoid justifying himself in the matter to which she referred, the treatment of the Indians. He was not prepared to go into that subject at the moment. Sooner or later he would have to address it, but first he meant to express his honest resentment at the way he had been treated, something that still pained him deeply. With his eyes still lowered, he found the strength to reply:

"With all due respect, Your Majesty, I cannot believe that Bobadilla, your new governor, had such explicit orders from Your Majesty – "

"How dare you question my authority!"

"Never your *authority, Your Majesty! Never! Only*

Bobadilla's arrogance and total disrespect toward me! To be placed under arrest? Not given a chance to speak for myself? Brought to Your Majesty in chains? No, no, I cannot believe even for a moment that those were your explicit orders!"

The Queen seemed ill at ease. She leaned lightly against her chair. "Not explicit orders perhaps, but, yes! you were to be brought back here to answer charges – "

"Charges??"

"Yes! Charges!. . . . For anyone to think we could have trusted so foolishly a man such as was being described to us – ! I had no choice. We had to recall you!"

"In chains??!!"

Isabella waved the question away. "That, I agree, was most unfortunate."

"At the request of my friends, the Captain agreed to set me free during the sea voyage, but I refused. I wanted Your Majesty to free me or tell me with your own lips that I was under arrest!" His head was throbbing. He took a deep breath.

The Queen spoke in a soothing voice, now. Her initial anger seemed to have subsided. "Well, the chains are off, aren't they!" She sat down in the same chair she had sat in when they last had met. Columbus took the chair opposite her, as he had on the earlier occasion. He raised his eyes finally, but fixed his gaze on the cross hanging over the door at the end of the room. The Queen continued:

"The new governor is efficient. He will maintain order on Hispaniola. We need more firmness and more show of strength now, especially since the Indians have become so hostile."

"I had succeeded in befriending them, you will recall. If the men had not gone off on their own, stealing pleasures and profit from those poor wretches, who at first had offered help, gifts, and friendship, I would not have had

104

to do what I did. It was inevitable under the circumstances."

"They murdered our men in Navidad, and they have set our people against one another. They have inflamed our leaders and brought chaos to our colony. Where our people are involved, I have no mercy, Columbus! . . . . Our new governor has restored order on the island. That's all that matters right now. Do you understand? Whatever the reasons, and they may be excellent ones, why you could not give enough time to that part of your job, conditions demand a change."

Finally, their eyes met: "I gave all the time in the world to that part of my job!" he whispered hoarsely, "And to much else! Just settling in was a formidable task. And just when I had succeeded in assessing the situation more realistically, after having made arrangements for a large shipment of pearls to be sent to Your Majesty, after bringing the insurrections to an end, I was told I don't serve well any more!"

The Queen shook her head impatiently. "The charge, Columbus, is not poor administration, although that too has come up, the charge is greed, theft, selfishness, unChristian motives – "

Unable to contain himself, Columbus jumped from his chair, paced to the door and back, as the words gushed out. "My orders were ignored! Contradicted! The men took Indian women and abused them, against my explicit orders! And when I tried to punish them, they ran off to be free of all restraints. They reported lies to Your Majesty, in order to cover their multitude of sins!"

Isabella frowned, as she watched him struggle to hold back more words. She waved him down again, and he resumed his seat, deflated. Slumped dejectedly where he sat, his hands between his knees, his chin resting on his chest, he seemed unaware of how he looked. He was the picture of utter *defeat.*

The Queen went on, almost lightly:

"Well, now that we have both aired our resentments, let's get down to the business at hand." She leaned forward trying to gain his attention. Slowly, Columbus raised his eyes. "You really have put me to a great deal of trouble and inconvenience, not to mention personal difficulties!" she began again. "I have always had faith in your honesty, Columbus. To change my opinion now would mean I was totally wrong about you all along. I like to think that is not the case. . . ."

Columbus was on the point of interrupting, but she held up her hand to stop him, and went on:

"But I must also tell you that my power to protect you is not what it was. We both must live with that fact. . . . All right. Let me tell you what I am prepared to do. We can't restore you to the rule of the islands; the King is absolutely firm on that point. He is determined to have the efficiency of a Bobadilla serve the Crown. Oh, it won't be Bobadilla – I still have some influence! – but it won't be you, either. You must live with that – "

"And what of the solemn terms of our agreement? That I remain Viceroy in all the lands I have claimed for the Crown in that part of the world? What of my family, my sons? I owe them something, surely!. . . . So many years in the service of Your Majesty! Am I to die a pauper then? My name forgotten?"

The Queen ignored the outburst and went on placidly: "You will retain your part of the gold and pearls brought here. Your back pay will be delivered to you. And, yes, I may have persuaded the King to let you have new fresh ships for a fourth trip!" She smiled hesitantly, waiting for a response.

"Your Majesty is most generous. . . ." He could not

keep the bitterness from his voice. The conditions laid down at the start obviously did not hold any longer. He was to receive back pay and a bonus, like any ordinary seaman. To take his mind off the enormity of what she had just told him, he fixed on her last words:

"The mainland is there, I know it! It's only a question of time!"

She picked up the cue quickly. "Yes, tell me about that. What about the mainland? I heard that a merchant, a Florentine who was working with my supervisor when the ships were being fitted recently, sailed to the Indies with a pilot of ours, Juan de la Cosa, and claims – "

" – claims to have discovered a new continent, yes! Amerigo Vespucci!" He spat out the words.

"Yes, that's the one!"

He leaned forward, careful not to betray the rage building up inside him. "I had written to your Majesty last year, you may recall," he began softly, "about coming from Trinidad to a coast where a large inland river emptied into the straits!" Before he could stop himself, he blurted out what was uppermost in his mind: "You see what comes of not keeping your – "

" – keeping my part of the bargain?. . . . Yes, well, things have changed, as you well know. The King and I feel that the Indies must be secured against any trespassing by other nations. It is essential that we put more people out there. You couldn't possibly have continued exploring alone, especially with your other duties on Hispaniola. Your glory will not diminish because we send other capable explorers to continue your work, study the region more thoroughly. Too much is at stake. Surely, you can understand that!" Columbus stared at her but said nothing. Other ships were being prepared, he knew, and other captains had already been enlisted by the Crown, but they were both aware, also,

that Vespucci had sailed for Portugal and that the Portuguese were already in the area. If he had been given more time, more ships, if there hadn't been so many distractions and delays, he could have done much more by this time. . . .

The Queen went on: "And, well, we still haven't found India, have we? In the letters that have been circulating, Vespucci is said to have – "

He couldn't help interrupting. "All that I have reported so far indicates we have found the outer islands of Asia. India has to be somewhere to the west of them. I didn't realize there were so many islands, but India is there, just beyond them. All our maps and charts, all our data tell us that. I don't know what Vespucci has found, what he's talking about. All I know is that India is within our grasp!"

The Queen studied his face. He returned her look, hoping the turmoil inside him did not show in his eyes.

"Columbus," Isabella went on, "what if something were to happen to you? Oh, we have all your charts and maps and notes, we could not have done anything without those. You've traced new routes for us, noted the hazards along the way, all that and much more! For that too, we owe you a tremendous debt of gratitude. . . ."

He pursued his own track doggedly: "I had written to Your Majesty about Paria, about Trinidad, the mainland just beyond, my plans for exploring that entire southernmost region – "

"Yes, yes, I just told you, you'll be going back with fresh ships to do that."

"People like Vespucci create . . . ambiguities! *But aside from that, our pact was that I alone should explore the region, once land was found, that I, I alone would be in charge!"*

Isabella was clearly annoyed by his refusing to let

108

go of the subject. "You tax my patience, Columbus! Thank God, no one is present to witness your manner of addressing me!"

He cursed his temper and met her angry look with imploring eyes. "It's not easy to see all one's plans reduced to rubble! After all the hardships, the privations, the sickness and disease, lack of provisions, not once thinking of myself, forging ahead always . . . always close to despair! It wasn't just . . . another job!"

The Queen stared at him for a moment then burst out laughing. Columbus was taken aback. "You do have a way with words, I must say! 'Just another job'! My friend, yours was genius! All the rest, that's 'just another job'! You have done remarkable things, Columbus. Leave the rest to the competent workers of the world. These changes were bound to happen. Leave the rest to others. Let go! . . . . Let go!"

Let go?? Nothing he had said seemed to have registered! He began once more, in a hoarse whisper: "You said I would rule the lands claimed in Your Majesty's name, for as long as I lived, and beyond that, my family would be given preference in all things relating to our agreement – "

She answered sharply this time. "If you must know, Columbus, it wasn't exactly my doing! I am a Queen, but I do have to answer to others. Even a Queen has to compromise from time to time. In this case, however, I finally had to agree with the reasoning behind our decisions. Things have changed. Circumstances call for new plans, more efficient strategies – "

"Even the Portuguese would never have treated the discoverer of the Indies in such a way!!" He hardly recognized the sound of his voice. The Queen stood up and glared at him. Columbus rose quickly. They stood facing one another, scarcely a foot apart.

"How dare you speak of the Portuguese in my

presence! They betrayed you! Oh, I know all about that, how they sent out ships with your charts and notes to guide them, to try to beat you to it! Yes, and how they turned back, too. And how you fled from Portugal because your life was in danger! You have gone too far, Columbus, too far!"

She seemed spent as she resumed her seat. Columbus remained standing, rooted to the spot. The Queen watched him in silence as he turned to her slowly and knelt before her.

"I beg Your Majesty to consider my state of mind. I am devastated by what has happened. I thought I could rely on the gold and honors promised me, to take care of my family over the years. I thought my family could trust me with their lives and futures! Instead, my sons will be disinherited. . . . !"

"Why do you exaggerate all that I say, Columbus! I know how much you have sacrificed and what this means to you. No, I'll be honest, I think it means more to you than I can begin to grasp. But I too have a job. I must do what is right for the future of Spain. You will not suffer because of our expansion in the Indies. But neither will I allow you to stand on agreements that have in effect been nullified by the greatness of the enterprise! We need at least a hundred of you, Columbus! One of you is no longer enough!"

She waited for him to say something. When he remained silent, she sighed softly, closed her eyes and leaned her head against the back of the chair, before continuing.

"I too am getting old, tired. Ever since the conquest of Granada – I tell you this as a friend – I have not been myself. I long for peace, rest. . . ." She opened her eyes only to meet a hard unfriendly stare. "You have sons, Columbus," she went on quickly, rising as she spoke, as though to bring the meeting to an end. "Let them take over. There is still much they can do. . . ."

"What guarantees do they have, my sons!" he burst

out helplessly, unable to stop the huge swell of despair that threatened to drown his soul. He rose quickly to his feet. "I must rest, you tell me. We are getting old, you say. I waited seven years before you told me I could sail. And I have carried on my work for almost another ten years. I am not an old man, but I have been forced to waste much precious time. And though still not an old man, I must let go and place my sons into the hands of the enemy!"

He watched abjectly as the Queen stood rigidly before him, her anger contained but obvious in her eyes, her expression. Columbus could only wait for the moment to pass. After a few seconds, Isabella hurried from the room.

Back in his quarters he groaned, remembering those last words. Things were bad enough, without his insulting the Queen by bringing up the Portuguese! He had known, even as he spoke, that he had alienated her, that he had done irreparable damage. . . . To have spoken like that to the Queen! The only person who had ever truly believed in him. . . . And yet, . . . and yet, . . . hadn't she too turned against him?

Suddenly the words of Pinzon, in the crazy dream he'd had, came back to him. The man had been right in that, at least. Never trust anyone!

Chapter Seven

THE FOURTH JOURNEY: SHATTERED DREAMS

Columbus had now been divested of his power and authority in Hispaniola; parts of the original agreement had more than once been reclaimed by the Crown; access to the colony he had founded was forbidden him; even his service as a sea captain was no longer required, since the routes he had discovered were now open to other experienced navigators. While he lingered in Spain, the seas he had sailed and tracked for the first time were in fact being explored by France, England, and Portugal, as well as Spain. He had become expendable. For the Sovereigns, he had become a nuisance.

Adjusting to the endless delays and biding his time in the hopes that the Sovereigns would address his complaints and restore to him what they had taken away, Columbus stood his ground for two years. The King and Queen finally ordered him to continue his explorations and provided him with four caravels for a fourth trip. They were relieved to see him go.

On May 9, 1502, the small fleet sailed out of Cadiz with 150 men, including the Admiral's son, Fernando, and his brother Bartholomew, both of whom had accompanied him to Spain. They stopped briefly for food and supplies in Martinique and on June 24 reached the southern coast of Puerto Rico. Five days later, they arrived at Santo Domingo. There — in spite of the royal order prohibiting him from landing in the colony, except in a real emergency — Columbus sent word to Ovando, the governor who had replaced Bobadilla, that one of the ships was not sailing well and needed to be replaced. No other reference has been found, before or after, to this "emergency." It may or may not have been a pretext to see for himself whether he still had friends on the island, now that the Sovereigns had shown signs of renewed support by sponsoring this fourth trip. Perhaps he wanted to check out the condition of the colonists, whether or not Ovando really had restored order, if the new settlement was truly prospering. Whatever the reason, Ovando took the request as a ploy to gain access again to Santo Domingo, and possibly spark new trouble by his presence, so he sent Columbus a peremptory order to move on — even though Columbus had warned him that a big storm was coming.

He had, in fact, strongly urged Ovando to delay the departure of thirty-two ships bound for Spain, carrying important dignitaries and a cargo of gold that today would be worth around forty-million dollars. Ovando, who saw nothing but clear skies above him and who no doubt found pleasure in any excuse to exert his authority and humiliate Columbus, laughed at the suggestion that a storm was brewing and of course did nothing.

The thirty-two ships left, headed for Spain. Columbus, who read in the changes in the air and the sea the same peculiarities he had noted just before a hurricane hit, at the time of his second trip, quickly took his four caravels to a small-protected port he had discovered earlier, Puerto Escondato (Hidden Port).

A short distance out, the fleet bound for Spain ran into the storm that Columbus had predicted. Twenty ships and at least 500 people went down. Some of the ships found temporary shelter along the southeastern coast of the island; four ships managed to make it back back to Santo Domingo; only one ship reached Spain. On that one ship, as fate would have it, was the gold Bobadilla had taken from Columbus, when he stripped him of titles and property before sending him back to Spain in chains, the gold that he had subsequently been ordered to return to the Admiral and was now waiting for Columbus in Spain.

Among those lost at sea were a number of Columbus's loyal friends, including his faithful former second-in-command, Antonio de Torres, as well as the trouble-maker Roldán, and Bobadilla, the former governor, who had done so much to humiliate Columbus and undermine his influence.

That Columbus had come out of this disaster unscathed did not go unnoticed. In time, people began to wonder how he was able to predict the terrible storm that destroyed almost an entire fleet of thirty-two ships. They wondered too how he had managed to find safe haven for his own ships. They marveled at the coincidence that the one ship that made it safely back to Spain happened to be carrying only that

114

portion of the gold that was earmarked for *him*. Speculation grew; rumors proliferated.

Columbus was a witch!

If he ever learned about this new title, it was much later, for on July 14, he was headed out to sea again, this time sailing southwest. His only concern now was finding the strait that would enable him to sail on to India.

He followed the curving coastline on the east. At Guanaja Island, not far from Honduras, he came into contact with the Chontal Mayas, who arrived in a large canoe, over forty feet long, with over three dozen men, women and children on board. He learned that they sailed regularly up and down the Yucatán peninsula, trading along the way. They traveled as far as Guatamala and Honduras. Guanaja Island was one of their trading posts.

Columbus was very much impressed by these newcomers, especially by a system of currency they had developed, using cacao beans. He noted too that the goods they offered were handcrafted with great skill. And, unlike other Indians, they covered most of their bodies. These were not the rough primitives he had met until then. Still, he was not surprised to find, in these new areas, more advanced people; it simply confirmed his belief that he was on the right track. India was not far off.

What would have surprised him would have been to learn that the goods the Mayas brought on these trading expeditions came from the plateaus of Mexico, and that just beyond that body of land was another great ocean that would have to be crossed before reaching India.

He treated the Mayas with courtesy and respect — which may seem to contradict his earlier and continued abuse of other Indians, but perhaps this can be explained, in part at least, by his wanting to keep on friendly terms with people who might eventually lead him to the fabled treasures reported by Marco Polo. When they left to continue their trading rounds, Columbus seriously considered following them, to see where they came from, where they actually lived. In the end, he chose to keep to his original plan of finding the strait that led to India. It was his overriding concern; the primary goal he set for himself on this fourth journey. Nothing would interfere with it.

Had he obeyed his impulse and followed the Mayas to their home base, he would have been the first European to reach Mexico. Instead, he pursued his quest for the elusive strait. Along the way, he took formal possession of Honduras. This turned out to be an important claim, for it gave Spain control of the entire region of what we now know as Central America.

After many storms and difficulties, he reached the point where the coastline begins to turn southward by slow degrees. He sailed past Nicaragua and Costa Rica and, on September 25, reached a sunny island full of palm trees, with all sorts of fauna and animals, including a strange bird "with feathers like wool" — no doubt a turkey. He also noticed that the gold ornaments worn by the Indians were skillfully worked and that they had built an entire structure out of wood and had raised some elaborate burial sites as well — additional signs of a more advanced people, the kind he had expected all along. Columbus named the place The Orchard.

Continuing southeast, along the curving coastline, he came to a channel very much like the one he had found in Trinidad. This one too was difficult to negotiate, and he gave it the same name as the other: The Dragon's Mouth. It led to Cerabora Bay. He knew it couldn't be the Bay of Bengal, but the signs again convinced Columbus he was very close to his goal. To add to his expectations and excitement, he found the Indians there all wore ornaments made of the purest gold.

Sailing south, he came to another bay (later named Bahia de Almirante) and two channels with many islets heavy with mangroves and other vegetation. The wider channel, now known as Split Hill Channel, raised expectations again. It led into a body of salt water, where the movement of the waves suggested an open sea on both sides. Columbus was now certain he had found the passage to India, but once again he was to be disappointed: after two days exploring the shore, he realized he had entered a salt-water lagoon.

This, as it turned out, was the critical point in the fourth and final journey of exploration. By October 16, 1502, almost ten years to the day after his first landing in the Caribbean, sick and disillusioned, Columbus

117

gave up forever his quest for the strait that would take him into the Indian Ocean. He never mentions the matter again, and no clear explanation has ever been found in any of his writings to account for this radical decision.

The condition of his ships may have been a factor. They were in serious disrepair. The storm they had encountered off the coast of Hispaniola, when they first set out, and the eighty-eight days of further storms along the way, had severely damaged them. By now, the vessels were also riddled with woodworm. He had already lost the Gallega because of it. A second ship had been lost when it was torn from its moorings during a storm and crashed into a third. The two ships left were taking in more and more water. Without the proper materials, he could not begin to repair anything. Many of the instruments were damaged also. It would have been suicide to attempt an extended journey under such appalling conditions.

Having to forego his quest must have been a cruel blow indeed if it meant abandoning a second and equally compelling reason for this last journey. Although no public or private admission has ever been found to support the idea, it has been suggested that both the Queen and Columbus had something bigger in mind, when the Admiral set out on his fourth journey: the circumnavigation of the globe, from east to west.The first leg of such a journey had already been accomplished by 1492. This time, he would come full circle. With seaworthy ships, he would sail south after leaving India, retracing the route of Vasco da Gama, who had reached it in May 1498 by sailing west to east around the Cape of Good Hope. Columbus would have continued up along the western coast of Africa, a trade route the Portuguese had established years earlier, and reached Spain from below. He would have completed Vasco da Gama's journey in reverse, sailed from Spain to the Indies, from there across the western strait to India, from there back to Spain. It would have been his culminating achievement.

It never happened, of course. Instead, he spent the next two and a half months sailing along the coast of what today is Panama, collecting gold. During this time, he made very few notes or observations in his journals. On January 7, 1503, he entered a lagoon and anchored there to trade for gold, since the entire area had proved to be the richest source yet of the precious metal. He also thought another Spanish colony would do well there; but when the Indians understood that the intruders were about to take over their land, they attacked, and a series of bloody battles followed. Columbus decided it was time to head back.

With the remaining two ships, now badly leaking and often swept off course by unfamiliar currents and huge winds, he barely made it into Puerto Bueno, in Jamaica, a place he had found when he first visited the island almost a decade earlier. There he was destined to remain for a full year. The ships, no longer seaworthy, had been beached; those parts not wholly destroyed by wormwood or damaged by the storms were

119

being used as makeshift living quarters.

Reduced to such conditions, with food dwindling fast, the men — many of whom were ravaged by illness and disease — grew weaker every day. All the while, the Indians, at first cooperative, grew increasingly hostile and often attacked the stranded ships. Columbus finally had to ask for volunteers to try getting word of their sorry plight to those on Hispaniola. A man named Diego Mendez accepted the charge. He fitted out, as best he could, one of the large Indian canoes Columbus had brought back and, together with a few other men, left to cross the stormy sea between Jamaica and Hispaniola.

As months went by, hopes for the success of Mendez's desperate venture diminished. The men who still had strength to do so, complained more and more openly. One day, a group of them mutinied. They stole several of the large canoes Columbus had brought back and set out for Hispaniola on their own. Bad weather soon forced them back, but not to the ships. Instead, they hid the canoes, hoping to make another attempt at the first possible opportunity, and went about raiding Indian villages, stealing food and whatever else they needed. To clear themselves of any wrongdoing, should they ever be held accountable, they told the Indians they victimized that they were following orders from the Admiral.

For Columbus and the rest of the men on the stranded ships, the future looked more and more grim with every passing day. The Indians, tired of providing for so many extra mouths and enraged by the cruel, reckless and licentious behavior of those who had abandoned the ships and were now roaming at will, turned hostile. It was no longer safe for anyone to leave the ships for whatever reason.

Ill and confined to his bed a good deal of the time, Columbus nevertheless came up with an ingenious remedy to win back the Indians. One of the books he had with him and often consulted listed a lunar eclipse for the night of February 29. Just before the event, Columbus sent word to the Indians that unless they provided food, water, and other necessities, as before, they would be severely punished by the gods. That night, he told them, they would be left in total darkness: the moon would be taken away from them. The Indians, needless to say, did not take it seriously; but when the eclipse began and the moon indeed started to disappear, they quickly sent word to the Admiral, begging him to intercede for them with the gods. Columbus replied that he would need time to convince the deities. When the moon began to appear again, he sent word that he had succeeded in getting the gods to relent.

The Indians, who a short time earlier had been ready to attack and kill the Spaniards at the first possible opportunity, now gladly did what was asked of them. Columbus had found a way out of what had seemed, until then, a hopeless predicament.

He knew it could be only a temporary respite. The crucial question, on which so much depended, still remained: had Mendez reached

Hispaniola? Or would they all die on Jamaica, lost forever, forgotten by the world? The answer finally came in the shape of a small brigantine that kept a certain distance and eventually sent someone in a boat with a message for the Admiral, a message to be delivered only to Columbus and only from aboard the boat which carried it. No one, including the messenger, was to set foot on the stranded ships.

To his dismay, Columbus learned that the brigantine had come only to deliver a side of beef and some wine — hardly enough to feed all the men one full meal. The message delivered to him was even more unsettling: the governor would send a ship when one became available.

He hurriedly wrote a reply to Ovando, thanking him for the supplies (careful not to mention their paucity), commending Mendez and his men for their determination and courage, explaining the dire circumstances in which he and those with him found themselves, the dangers surrounding them. The letter was entrusted to the messenger, who quickly returned to his ship. Soon after, the Brigantine sailed off.

Columbus was just as disturbed as the rest of his men at what they had all witnessed. When the others raised the obvious question, he tried to reassure them by suggesting that a brigantine was too small a ship to carry them all back to Hispaniola. No one really accepted that answer, least of all Columbus. A brigantine might be small, but it could have carried back at least those men who were dying or in urgent need of medical attention. There was more behind what Columbus saw as an open display of Ovando's arrogance. The governor was clearly set on destroying him, even though the Queen had given unambiguous orders that Columbus was to be treated at all times with respect and dignity — in spite of the restrictions placed on him.

Columbus kept such thoughts to himself, but he could not help thinking that Ovando had no intention of sending a vessel to rescue them — at least not for a while. Maybe he was delaying purposely, so that by the time he did send a ship Columbus and all his men would be found conveniently dead. . . .

On Hispaniola, where he patiently waited for Ovando to send a ship to rescue the stranded men, Diego Mendez too came to the conclusion that Ovando was not about to do anything. Taking matters into his own hands, he bought and fitted at his own expense one of the smaller ships that had recently arrived from Spain and sent it on to Jamaica. Ovando, realizing that Mendez's stories of the hardships Columbus and his men had endured was turning public opinion against him, quickly fitted a ship of his own and sent it to catch up with the other.

The sick and bedraggled band arrived on Hispaniola on June 29. Ovando, still bent on humiliating Columbus by exerting his authority over him, immediately freed the leaders of the mutiny, who had been brought back in chains to be tried and punished. It was an act of defiance that could not possibly be misinterpreted. When the Admiral protested, Ovando turned deaf ears to his arguments. Columbus could do nothing but wait for the next available ship to take him back to Spain, where he would report Ovando's ill-treatment to the Sovereigns. He planned also to urge them, once again, to restore to him what was rightfully his.

When he arrived in Spain, on November 7, 1502, he did not know that the Queen was gravely ill. Only later did he learn that she had died on November 26. In the months that followed, he made repeated efforts to gain an audience with the King, but it wasn't until May of 1505 that Ferdinand finally agreed to see him.

At best distant and aloof, Ferdinand greeted Columbus coldly, listened to his request for an arbiter to settle his claims, but made no commitment. When an arbiter was at last agreed on, the King firmly rejected any attempt that would make him honor the original agreements. It soon became evident that had he been able to do so without incurring the criticism and displeasure of his subjects, who commiserated with the sufferings undergone by Columbus for so many years, the King would readily have stripped him even of what remained of his hard-won gains.

Columbus remained at Court, then in Segovia, at least through August 25, when records show he signed his will before a notary. By then it was clear that he could expect nothing more from the King. Ferdinand stood on privilege; the last word was his. Totally defeated and humiliated, worn out by illness, Columbus finally left for Valladolid, where he died on May 20, 1506, his sons and a few other family members and close friends at his bedside. Except for the few who witnessed his death, it went unnoticed. He was fifty five (if indeed he was born in 1451); but even if we accept 1446 as the earlier date of his birth, he was no more than sixty when he died, worn out in his prime by prolonged physical and mental suffering.

By the time of his death, his resources had been greatly depleted, but he was never a poor man. Still, the promises made and ratified by the Crown in a number of agreements that had constantly been revised over the many years had significantly diminished the expectations that had been ratified early on. In the first binding contracts between the Sovereigns and Columbus, he was to receive — among other things — the hereditary titles of Admiral and Viceroy of all the seas, lands, and islands he discovered; and, after deducting costs, one tenth of all the gold, silver, pearls, precious stones, spices, and other goods found, collected, received by barter or acquired or gained in any other way, anywhere in his admiralty. In addition he would receive one-eighth of the total profits taken in. The terms of those original agreement would have assured an enormous fortune for his heirs; he could easily have emerged as the founder of the richest corporation in the world, matched only by the multinationals of the twentieth century.

Understandably, he wanted the original terms of the agreement restored. In the light of subsequent events, the Sovereigns, on their part, realized they could not and should not do so. In the wake of the excitement generated by the plan Columbus had first presented to them, hearing about the rich possibilities and the incredible potential they might indeed realize as a result of a new west-east route to India, the King and Queen were at first prepared to be generous. The enormous risk Columbus was taking deserved rich rewards. If he never returned, they would not lose much in the investment they had made; if he succeeded, there would be more than enough profits to go around. At the time the initial agreements were drawn, the Sovereigns simply had not faced the realities of a situation yet to be fully defined.

In reality, costs had quickly escalated and the treasury was putting out much more money than anticipated to cover delays, to provide for the colonists, to send supplies and ships on a regular basis (the plantations were not yet yielding much), to insure protection against the Indians, who had soon after the first encounters predictably turned hostile. There were of course profits on the other side of the ledger, including the Indian slave market (which insured workers for the mines and plantations), new deposits of high-quality gold and pearls (which promised large yields), the claims to lands that might easily produce new and unknown riches. Potential profits might turn out to be enormous, but actual costs were significantly depleting the treasury.

Given the enormous expenses and the still uncertain returns, it was not surprising that the King and Queen should have periodically reviewed and made changes in the original contract they had signed with Columbus. They realized soon enough that they had turned over too large a share to one man, even if he had found for Spain new lands and the routes needed to lay permanent claim to them. His titles especially had suffered later scrutiny; in particular, the hereditary position of Viceroy of all the colonies. The Crown was right, of course, in protecting its own interests. The dialectic of history forces such decisions, reality makes us accept the need for them. Columbus, however, felt he had been betrayed and pressed his claims to the very end — without much success. He did manage to get permission to entail his estate.

In his will, he named his son Diego as his immediate heir, the inheritance to be passed down through the legitimate line, but always with Fernando's interests well protected. Should Diego's line fail, the estate would revert to his brothers and their male successors. If the male lines all failed, the estate would then pass on to the women. The document also called for his executors to donate one tenth of the estate to charities and to make certain sums available to Genoa, should his native city ever need help. Moreover, periodic investments were to be made through the Banco San Giorgio, to be used eventually to help in the recovery of the

Holy Sepulcher, once that project got under way.

With efficient foresight, Columbus had set down the conditions that would insure the continuation of his personal legacy. He could not possibly have foreseen, much less insured, the future of the claims he had made for Spain in the course of his explorations. The Portuguese, who had first instilled in others the passion for discovery, had, in the wake of Columbus, soon found their way across the Atlantic. Spain watched warily, soon raised objections. Tensions between the two countries might easily have turned into open warfare had they not agreed, early in 1493, to appeal to the Pope — at the time, Alexander VI, of the powerful Borgia family. The answer was the Bull of Demarcation or The Treaty of Tordesillas of May 4, 1493 (later revised). The Pope drew an imaginary line in the Atlantic from north to south, allowing Spain all their claims west of that line and Portugal, whatever claims they made east of the line. The most dramatic result of this agreement would prove to be Portugal's acquisition of Brazil.

The Pope's decision also served to temporarily restrain England (still a Catholic country) from explorations — but only in that disputed part of the world. Inspired by the success of Columbus and consumed with a desire to do some "notable thing," John Cabot — born in Genoa, a one-time resident of Venice, and at this time a naturalized citizen of Bristol, England — applied to King Henry VII for a patent to sail and trade with other countries. He was granted such a patent in 1496; in May of 1497, he sailed from Bristol and touched land a month later at Cape Breton, or, as some still believe, at Labrador or Newfoundland. He thought he had touched the easternmost coast of Asia, just as Columbus believed he had reached the outer islands of Japan.

He was rewarded by the King, who was certain that Cabot's claim would open up new and profitable trade routes for England, and was hailed by the public as a national hero — an honor Columbus (although royally treated) never won among the Spaniards.

In May of 1498, four months before Columbus left Spain on his third voyage, Cabot sailed out again, this time with six ships, on his second journey of exploration. With him was one of his sons, Sebastian, who later would reach the Northwest Passage. One of the ships headed for Ireland; the others continued westward and were never heard from again. One theory has it that Spain, already challenging the English claims, at some point came into possession of documents recording Cabot's second voyage and destroyed them to prevent others from learning about it. Whatever the reason, Cabot no longer appears in any records.

By now, Portugal was well into the area where Spain still dominated. Following Vasco da Gama's opening of the west-east route to India, Pedro Alvarez Cabral was given charge, in March, 1500, of three ships to test that route. At one point, for whatever reason, Cabral chose to shift from a southerly to a westerly course. On April 22, he reached and named Vera Cruz (later Santa Cruz). On May 1 he took formal possession, for Portugal, of the land mass he had found within the prescribed limits of the Bull of Demarcation: Brazil.

Most historians agree that sooner or later the Portuguese would have discovered the "new world" without the help of Columbus. But the fact remains that Columbus was indeed the first to open up the route for other nations. Sailing down the western coast of Africa, Cabral knew that there was land in the west — Columbus had proved it — and detoured in that direction, hoping to find more. Within the larger picture, he too deserves credit, as the discoverer of Brazil. In the measured words of Justin Winsor: "Columbus sought India and found America without knowing it. Cabral, bound for the Cape of Good Hope, stumbled on Brazil, and preëmpted the share of Portugal in the New World as Da Gama had already secured it in Asia. Thus the African route revealed both Cathay and America."*

Columbus himself never realized what he had stumbled on. He never suspected he had come upon a great continent, unknown to the Europeans until then. Almost to the very end, he believed he had found the outer islands of Japan and that in time he would find his way through that maze of islands and get to the passage that would take him to India. That fixed goal sapped his energies and proved an obstacle to larger hopes for Spain. The Portuguese were more successful in exploiting their claims and colonizing their lands: they had a more lasting impact. But it was left for another Italian, a Florentine, to suggest for the first time the staggering implications of what Columbus never seemed to have realized and Cabral had no reason to question. Assertions of a 1497 voyage by Vespucci have pretty well been discredited, but there are enough documents and clear references that place him in the Caribbean in 1499. One reliable source is Alonzo de Ojeda, who had sailed with Columbus on the first journey. As a witness in a legal matter relating to opposing claims, Ojeda testified that both Juan de la Cosa and Vespucci sailed with him in 1499. Vespucci may or may not have heard about Cabral's discovery of Brazil when on May 1, 1501, Cabral's fleet, returning from India, and the ship on which Vespucci was sailing happened to come together at Cape Verde Islands. Letters attributed to Vespucci himself, written in 1503, in which the writer describes how they reached the coast of Cape St. Roque on August 17, 1501, seem authentic. In that document, we learn that on August 28, they came to Cape St. Augustine and by April 28 had worked their way to a latitude of 52° south. From there they headed east again and sailed back along the coast of Africa. They arrived in Lisbon on September 7, 1501.

The original Italian text of the letters is lost, and it is not certain what Vespucci called the area described in it; or if he gave it a name of any kind; but the Latin version which soon appeared carried the name *Mundus Novus*. In it, Vespucci speaks of a land mass that could not be Asia, that it had to be an entirely new continent, unknown to Europeans until then.

Mundus Novus went through several editions in Germany and France. Soon after, translations into Italian, French, and Dutch began circulating throughout Europe. A curious development was that the new maps began showing a continuous land mass north of the Caribbean, but no clear source has ever been found for what appears to have been conjecture rather than substantiated fact. Most writers on the subject claim that the Portuguese were very likely the source of the rumors that occasioned those additions, since they were the ones who welcomed new maps, in order to support their legitimate claims in the south, while Spain made every effort to prevent the spread of new information in order to confuse the issue of Portuguese claims. In any case, enough data (true or rumored) seems to have been collected by then to convince mapmakers that there was land north of where Columbus had made his discoveries and very likely south of that area, as well.

It was in one of the new maps that the Florentine's name first appeared. No one could possibly have foreseen the historic consequences of that simple notation.

The story is, that Duke Rene of Lorraine, a man of culture who followed with great interest the many new advances being made in science, had set up within his jurisdiction, in the tiny village of St. Dié, a small college, where he invited scholars and scientists. One of the people in residence there was Martin (or Walter) Waldseemüller, a young scholar who had been brought in as Professor of Geography and who was also skilled at drawing maps. Waldseemüller, a great admirer of Vespucci, was about to publish a very small volume of his own, *Cosmographiae introductio*, and decided to add, at the end, Vespucci's letters. Originally addressed to Piero Soderini, then *gonfaloniere* of Florence, Vespucci's letters had been circulating among a small group of people interested in what they contained. One copy had reached another Florentine, working in Paris, who showed them to a young professor of Latin from St. Dié. The letters were entrusted to him and brought back to France, where they were translated into Latin, under the title *Mundus Novus*, and given to Waldseemüller for his new book.

In his book, Waldseemüller also included a new map he had drawn, showing all recent discoveries. Only a few hand-drawn copies had been circulated locally before *Cosmographiae introductio*, appeared; but with the publication of the little treatise, in 1507, Vespucci's account and the map drawn by Waldseemüller began to attract wide attention. The author had explained the notation he had made with these words: "the fourth part of the world having been discovered by Americus, it may be called Amerige, i.e. Americus' land or America." In 1509, he further explained that the feminine form was in keeping with the names Europa and Asia. The name America soon appeared on other maps. By 1522 it had found its way into an updated edition of Ptolemy's *Geographia*.

There is nothing to suggest that Vespucci himself made any deliberate effort to gain notoriety or to immortalize himself in this way. That he deserves the recognition given him cannot ever be seriously doubted: among other things, he also established, in 1503, the first permanent colony of Europeans in South America. When he died in 1512, his fame was established; his honors intact; his legacy unquestioned — a far cry from the unhappy fate of Columbus, who summed up (according to Washington Irving) what he had won for all his hard labors as "chains for a crown, a prison for a world."

THE COLUMBUS LEGACY

History tells us that the Phoenicians may have been the first to sail the Mediterranean. After them, came the Arabs, whose raiding expeditions made them aware of the lands on the northern shores of that body of water. The Norsemen, in their time, seem to have reached the North American shore, but they left no permanent colony or no trace of any prolonged activity there: settlements were found, instead, in Greenland and Iceland.

But it was Christopher Columbus who deliberately took up the challenge of crossing the vast unchartered western Atlantic – something that, recorded history tells us, no one before him had done. The plan was not for sporadic hunting or other seasonal activities, but to establish a permanent base and develop economic resources for long-term development and expansion. Finding gold was only the beginning.

When it came to sailing into the unknown ocean sea, he was without question the perfect man for the job. He had courage, confidence in his skills, and an uncanny instinct with regard to sailing and matters related to the sea. His voyages into the North Atlantic, down the western coast of Africa, in the Mediterranean, had prepared him well. He could read maps and charts better than anyone else. His own calculations were based on what was known about the earth at that time and also on Marco Polo's account of the lands he visited in the Orient. Using the charts and maps available to him, and drawing upon his own estimates of distances, Columbus proved to be amazingly accurate. Cipango and the islands off the mainland of Asia should have been where he found, instead, the islands of the Caribbean. What barred the way to Asia was a large land mass, taking up roughly a third of the planet, an entire continent no one in Europe had ever heard about. If that body of land had not been there, Columbus would indeed have landed near Japan, the fabled Cipango Marco Polo had written about.

In his own mind, Columbus never seems to have solved the puzzle of where he had landed. He may have lost faith, at some point, in what he had expected to find; but there is no indication in any of his writings or any other records that he ever conceived the possibility of having come upon a totally different land mass, islands unknown to Europeans before then. If he suspected anything of the kind, he never spoke of it, although at times he seems no longer sure about his surroundings.

He may not have been sure where he had landed, but Columbus was confident in his own experience and training. He was a master at dead reckoning and could read the signs around him with accuracy. The title "Admiral of the Ocean Sea" was well deserved: not only did he find lands

Europe knew nothing about at the time; he also established for all who sailed after him two important routes: the one that would take them to those lands and a second route for getting back. For, as Columbus had realized, on the first return trip, they had to avoid the trade winds that always blew westward.

He was the first, also, to recognize what we have come to know as the Gulf Stream, the first to cross and describe in detail the Sargasso Sea. He deserves immense credit for venturing into the strangling weeds of that body of water, ignoring superstitions and old legends, in order to describe the phenomenon accurately for later maritime traffic. His venture into the Sargasso Sea must be rated as a major contribution to the history of navigation.

But his greatest claim to fame and glory is the fact that he crossed a vast uncharted body of water at a time when even the best seamen – the Portuguese – were not prepared to do so. Their habit was to keep close to land, and they did just that in their explorations down the western coast of Africa.

He knew both greatness and oblivion. In the end, and at this distance in time, his life may be described most accurately as a Sophoclean unwinding into tragedy: like Oedipus, he takes on heroic proportions, in spite of poor judgment at times. He will always stand apart as the embodiment of the Renaissance spirit of discovery, the man who imbued others with a sense of wonder about the Unknown and a desire to explore it, and – by his own fearless example – gave others the courage to satisfy that yearning.

(OR, AS WASHINGTON IRVING, MIGHT HAVE TOLD IT:)
What was it like? Magic! Incredible! Unbelievable! They were gods to the Indians but friends to Kings and Queens . . . which is much more valuable! Think of it! The Queen of Spain and the immigrant from Genoa, who

discovered a whole new world and didn't know it! Who would have predicted it! Of course, the whole thing was extraordinary from the start. What other single event in the history of the world can compare? . . . The space program? No, no. That's . . . technology! What's technology? . . . Technology is . . . TECHNOLOGY! The Greeks knew all about the atom, but they didn't have the technology to do anything with it. . . . Did Einstein care about technology?

Sorry, I haven't introduced myself. I'm Washington Irving. . . . Ah, you think I wrote only about Rip Van Winkle? That was nothing compared to the story of Columbus. I spent many years in Spain, you know. Read everything I could lay my hands on, visited more places than you can name looking for documents, books, letters, journals, his meetings with the King and Queen, the accounts of people who knew him like Las Casas, Peter Martyr, and all the others. I found myself drawn into that story more and more. It was irresistible. I was probably the first to write about Columbus in English. I love history! I think Columbus felt the same way about discovery! The sea was his home. On land, he was restless and often ineffectual. But on a ship he proved himself, again and again, the best navigator of his time.

There's so much to tell! All I can do is remind you of some of the highlights of his unusual story.

He was definitely Genovese. Don't let anybody tell you otherwise. There is too much idle speculation about his birth and much else; but documents do exist (including his will, where Genoa is provided for), and there are enough witnesses for us to be pretty sure about his place of birth. The year is not altogether certain, that's true, but most scholars have placed it in 1451. And we are also certain that around the age of fifteen he left Genoa to become a seaman, like his brother Bartholomew before him. Like the immigrants, who

followed him to the land he had first discovered for Europe,
he left his native country for greater opportunities, a better
life than Genoa could provide for those who made sailing
their business. That once great seafaring city-state – like
Venice, once-the uncontested Queen of the Adriatic – had
passed her prime. And she certainly could not fund the kind
of grand idea Columbus was hatching!

We also know that he married a Portuguese woman
and became a Portuguese citizen; that he spoke and wrote in
Portuguese but also taught himself Spanish while waiting
seven years at the Court for the King and Queen to decide on
his grand plan. We know he died in Valladolid and was
buried there; that later his body was taken for reinterment in
Seville. After that, things get very confused: the last burial
place is, in fact, still in question. Claims are made that he is
buried in Santo Domingo; others, that the body ended up in
Cuba; still others, that his bones were finally put to rest
permanently back in Spain. To this day, no one really knows
for certain where Columbus is buried. There is no question
that it was moved at least twice. Beyond that, we can only
guess where it finally ended up.

What was he like? He had a very good memory and
a disciplined mind. Very often, especially on that first historic
voyage, he had to rely on his instincts for the most part –
honed by long experience, of course – but his guesses, then
and later, always proved right. He recorded meticulously
everything around him. In the unfamiliar waters and lands
he found himself in, he learned to read strange and unusual
signs, noting with precision the currents, the winds, the
animals and plants, changes in the air and water and
atmosphere, the stars, everything. Almost to the end he kept
careful notes. You might say, he was his own expert computer
programmer.

In times of crises, he never failed his men or others

who depended on him. He dealt with the unexpected with determination and plenty of guts. No one was quite so fearless. He took on a dangerous mission that no one else dared and, in the course of it, not only found new lands, but also brought back news about the trade winds, and went out of his way to record the phenomenon of the Sargasso Sea and the Gulf Stream. And although he never actually realized he had found a body of land never mentioned before in recorded history, his calculations for reaching India by sailing west proved to be surprisingly accurate – for he would indeed have reached the outer islands of Japan if this great continent had not been in his way. All the information of the time showed the earth one-third less than the size we now know it to be. So, even in that large error, paradoxically, he was proved right. His journeys also bolstered the theory that the earth was round.

What else did he do?

He provided the impetus for further explorations. No doubt, sooner or later someone else would have done what Columbus did, as some observers have noted. But it was Columbus, not someone else, who accomplished what seemed an impossible feat.

Ripeness is all, as the poet tells us. It was the age of new hopes, new exciting possibilities and bold ventures in all fields – painting, sculpture, poetry, architecture, science – an age moved to re-examine the world with new eyes, with the kind of wonder and curiosity the Greeks had first shown. Against that background, Columbus emerges as the embodiment of the Renaissance spirit of discovery.

One can minimize his achievement and point out, as some have done, that he simply was at the right place at the right time. That's true, in a way; but without his particular training, his charts, maps, notes and other crucial data, men like John Cabot would not have sailed westward

139

into the North Atlantic and landed in Cape Breton; Cabral would not have hazarded the detour in the southern zone and come upon Brazil, on his way around the Cape of Good Hope; Vespucci would not have sailed down the eastern coast of that land mass in the south and recorded the possibility of a whole new continent. It might have happened, probably would have happened somewhere down the line, but it happened when it did and in the manner it did, only because of Columbus. He was the first.

Oh, he had his faults. He was tempted, like the rest of us. No, that's really not the proper word in this case. He wasn't greedy, like those around him. But promises had been made and retracted; honors had been given and taken away; contracts had been made and broken. He had a right to what had been promised him and, until his death, tried desperately to regain for his heirs what had been denied him. He did not succeed. In the end, he may have seen his life as a dismal failure.

From the start, things went wrong for him and led him into bad decisions. Unlike other colonies that eventually took root in the new world, those of Spain had an especially bad time of it. Columbus, who in addition to the original title of Admiral of the Ocean Sea was also given the title and responsibilities of Viceroy of all the lands he discovered, soon realized that he had to rely more and more on released criminals to work the mines and fields of Hispaniola. This proved a huge mistake. The men thus employed soon tired of taking orders and abandoned the colony to roam at will, raiding and pillaging wherever they went. It was a situation Columbus could not allow yet could not control effectively.

Circumstances also worked against him. He could not cope with the enormous problems of a new colony ravaged by malaria and other diseases, dependent on released criminals to work the land and the mines, powerless to deal

140

effectively with the deserters who victimized the Indians with impunity, unable to raise enough food to feed its growing population and often having to wait months for much-needed supplies from Spain. Columbus, as Viceroy of the colony, was overwhelmed by these difficulties. He tried his best to bring law and order to bear on such a situation; the fact that he had been absent for two years, exploring the seas, leaving his brother in charge, did not help matters.

He had to face other big troubles. The initial friendly relationship with the Indians soon had deteriorated; they were now enemies. Spain had, perhaps inadvertently, taken up the role of conqueror. And conquest means one side wins, the other loses. Eventually the Indians were subdued and made to work on the plantations and in the mines. But with the painful realization that he had not found the treasures of India, and with the yield from the plantations still not sufficient to feed the expanding colony, Columbus began to sell Indians as slaves in order to produce the gold he had promised the Sovereigns. The Queen objected at first; she wanted the Indians converted only. But her counselors persuaded her that the slave trade would provide much-needed revenue. Their arguments, in the light of the large losses already incurred in the colonies, were effective. She gave in.

The Indian slave trade certainly brought money to Spain, but it made things infinitely worse for Columbus on Hispaniola. He now had to fight off Indians at every turn — those who remained and were strong enough to do so. In the end, many tribes were wiped out because of the kind of life they were forced to endure. Such is the record: and it should not be altered or rewritten according to current standards and values. History does not judge. Our educated sensibilities tell us, rightly, that slavery is indeed reprehensible; history tells us that it is as old as the Greeks,

141

who (as far as we can tell) made slaves of all those captured in war; and as recent as the slave trade among Africans. Then too, the age of Columbus was not an age of democracy and personal freedom, as we have come to define those terms. Those are the facts. That it was a sorry decision, is just as obvious.

History also tells us that Columbus never knew what he had found. That's the bad news, in a way. The good news is that history is full of ironies and paradoxes that eventually sort themselves out. Only then, at a distance in time, do we see the large picture with clarity. Looking back on the story of Columbus, we are moved to wonder, rather than judgment.

An interesting footnote (I like trivia, don't you?) is that sixteen years to the day he died, on May 20, 1522, the armies of Charles of Spain invaded Italy and destroyed Genoa.

The historical facts are clear enough. Columbus was honored briefly, then forgotten and ignored. In his time, that is. He made four different trips of exploration in his efforts to find the strait that would take him through, to India, just beyond. Each time, those islands held him back, like a barrier! No way through!

But the most dramatic paradox in the entire story is that the continent Columbus set foot on – the first European to do so – was not named after him but after one of the navigators who followed in his wake: a Florentine who sailed for Portugal: Amerigo Vespucci.

As I said earlier: history is like that! Full of ironies!

EPILOGUE

It is a curious fact that Italian-Americans have come to honor Columbus, rather than Vespucci, as their national hero. Even more curious, as Justin

Winsor reminds us, is that although "Venice gave her Cabot to England, Florence bestowed Verrazano upon France, Genoa gave Columbus to Spain and Florence accredited her Vespucius to Portugal," the Italians who produced those pioneers never "secured in the New World a foothold for themselves."*

---

*Justin Winsor, *Christopher Columbus* (Connecticut, Longmeadow Press. rpt 1992, p. v.
